THE ULTIMATE STRASBOURG FRANCE TRAVEL GUIDE 2024

Comprehensive Guide to the Best Attractions, Local Experts Tips on a Budget Friendly Journey

MARK A. GUZMAN

Copyright © 2023 by Mark A. Guzman

All rights reserved. No part of this book may be reproduced in any form or by any electronic or mechanical means, including information storage and retrieval systems, without permission in writing from the author. The only exception is by a reviewer, who may quote brief passages in a review.

TABLE OF CONTENTS

INTRODUCTION... 7
CHAPTER 1: WELCOME TO STRASBOURG.... 13
   A Brief History of the City............................... 13
   Why Choose Strasbourg for Your Next Adventure.. 18
CHAPTER 2: PLANNING YOUR JOURNEY....... 23
   Best Times to Visit Strasbourg......................... 23
   Navigating Transportation: Getting In and Around... 30
   Visa Information and Travel Essentials........... 35
   Budget-Friendly Accommodations................... 39
CHAPTER 3: UNVEILING STRASBOURG'S CHARM... 45
   The Strasbourg Experience: Culture and Lifestyle... 45
   Exploring the Historic Districts........................ 51
   Must-Try Local Cuisine and Dining Hotspots.. 56
   Embracing the Strasbourg Lifestyle................ 62
CHAPTER 4: TOP ATTRACTIONS AND LANDMARKS... 69
   Strasbourg Cathedral: A Gothic Masterpiece. 69
   La Petite France: A Picturesque Canal District... 74
   The Strasbourg Museum Trail......................... 78
   Riverside Parks and Gardens,,,,.................... 83
CHAPTER 5: INSIDER TIPS FOR A MEMORABLE JOURNEY..................................... 89
   Local Experts' Insights.................................... 89

Hidden Gems: Off the Beaten Path.................95
Cultural Etiquette and Traditions...................100
Maximizing Your Experience on a Budget.... 106

CHAPTER 6: DAY TRIPS AND BEYOND..........112
Excursions to Nearby Villages.......................112
Wine Tasting in the Alsace Region................119
Outdoor Adventures: Hiking and Cycling Routes 124
Exploring Strasbourg's Surroundings............128

CHAPTER 7: SHOPPER'S PARADIDE............. 135
Strasbourg's Markets and Boutiques............ 135
Unique Souvenirs to Bring Home.................141
Shopping Districts for Every Budget............. 145

CHAPTER 8: NIGHTLIFE AND ENTERTAINMENT 151
Evening Strolls and Illuminated Landmarks.. 151
Trendy Bars and Cafés................................. 156
Live Music and Cultural Performances......... 160

CHAPTER 9: PRACTICAL TIPS AND RESOURCES... 165
Essential Travel Apps................................... 165
Safety Guidelines and Emergency Contacts 169
Sustainable Travel Practices.........................173
Q&A Section: Common Traveler Inquiries.... 178

CHAPTER 10: YOUR STRASBOURG ITINERARY 185
One-Day Whirlwind Tour............................... 185
Weekend Getaway Recommendations..........190
Extended Stay Adventures........................... 194

CONCLUSION...202

Final Thoughts and Reflections..................... 202
How to Stay Connected and Share Your
Strasbourg Experience..................................206

INTRODUCTION

Imagine entering a place where culture dances in the air you breathe, history whispers through every cobblestone, and every moment seems like it could be torn from a fairy tale. Welcome to Strasbourg, France, a mesmerizing city in the Alsace region known for its distinct and entrancing ambiance resulting from the blending of French and German influences.

Walk along the canals in the quaint Petite France neighborhood, where half-timbered homes with brightly colored flower arrangements create a scene straight out of a bygone period. Climb the spire of the magnificent Strasbourg Cathedral, a Gothic architectural marvel that looms over the city and provides breath taking sweeping views of the surroundings. Take in the lively Christmas markets, where the scent of gingerbread fills the air and dazzling lights create a mystical atmosphere.

Your Go-To Guide for an Unforgettable Adventure in Strasbourg

It might be difficult to find your way about Strasbourg, especially if you're a first-time visitor. Here's where "THE ULTIMATE STRASBOURG FRANCE TRAVEL GUIDE 2024" comes in handy, acting as your go-to guide for a smooth and remarkable trip to Alsace.

In-Depth Guide to the Greatest Attractions

This all-inclusive travel book shows you Strasbourg's undiscovered beauties and hidden secrets, taking you off the well-traveled tourist routes. Explore the city's gastronomic delights, lively arts scene, and rich history—all conveniently located at your fingertips.

Tips from Local Experts for an Affordable Trip

With insider tips and methods, you can maximize your experiences and minimize costs while embracing Strasbourg like a native. This book gives you the tools to explore Strasbourg on a budget, from using public transit to locating hidden gems for delicious Alsatian food.

Differences This Travel Guide Has From Others

"THE ULTIMATE STRASBOURG FRANCE TRAVEL GUIDE 2024" goes deeper than other travel books that simply list places, creating a tapestry that captures Strasbourg's character from its historical significance to its vibrant modern culture.

Reasons Why This Travel Guide Is Needed

This travel book is your ticket to an incredible Alsatian trip, regardless of whether you're an experienced tourist looking for new experiences or a first-time visitor eager to see Strasbourg's charms. It's the key that opens the city's mysteries and turns your trip from a typical vacation into an enchanted memory bank.

Set Out on an Exploration

Strasbourg waits to be discovered, ready to share its alluring appeal, with "THE ULTIMATE STRASBOURG FRANCE TRAVEL GUIDE 2024" serving as your guide. As you go out on a quest of exploration, let the city's rich history, lively culture, and mouthwatering cuisine captivate your senses.

Accept the Alsatian Spirit

Enjoy the friendliness of the people, tuck into the tastes of authentic Alsatian food, and take in the distinctive fusion of French and German influences of Strasbourg as you meander around its charming streets.

Make Lasting Memories

Strasbourg will enchant you with every step you take and every encounter you have, leaving you with lasting memories long after your trip is over. This travel guide is an invitation to explore Strasbourg's heart and soul—a city that will always have a particular place in your heart—rather than merely a book.

CHAPTER 1: WELCOME TO STRASBOURG

A Brief History of the City

The fascinating city of Strasbourg, located in the center of Alsace, France, has a complex and rich history that has been influenced by the ebb and flow of time and the collision of various civilizations. Its history is a tapestry woven with strands of French, Germanic, Roman, and Celtic influences, giving it a distinct character that has lasted for centuries.

Roman Basis: Argentoratum's Ascent

The city's history begins in 12 BC, when the Romans built Argentoratum, a military camp in a key location along the Rhine River. As an important defensive position against Germanic tribes, this strategically placed outpost developed into a bustling commercial hub that drew traders and merchants from all over the Roman Empire.

The Changing Terrain of the Early Middle Ages

The Alemanni, a Germanic tribe, and then the Merovingians ruled Strasbourg as the Roman Empire began to decline in the fifth century. The city's name changed during this time from Argentoratum to Strateburgum, which translates to "roadside town," indicating its significance as a hub for trade and transportation.

An Abundant Free City Under the Holy Roman Empire

After Strasbourg joined the Holy Roman Empire in the eighth century, the city saw rapid expansion and wealth. The city's strategic position and bishopric status enhanced its political and economic power. Strasbourg became a free imperial city in 1262, which gave it a great deal of independence and self-governance.

The French Connection: The Beginning of a New Era

In an attempt to increase his sphere of influence, Louis XIV of France conquered Strasbourg in 1681. This was a watershed in the city's history, as it led to a period of cultural and architectural change and its incorporation into the French kingdom.

France and Germany: Two Cities with Two Lives

After the Franco-Prussian War of 1870, Germany was once more granted possession of Strasbourg. The city's German background was once again evident at this time, as it was made the capital of the Reichsland of Alsace-Lorraine. Nevertheless, French rule over Strasbourg returned following World War I.

Global Conflicts and the Search for Harmony

Two catastrophic World Wars occurred in the 20th century, and Strasbourg saw occupation and fighting during those years. But the city came out of these tribulations resolved to advance harmony and peace. Strasbourg, a representation of European cooperation and unity, became the home of the Council of Europe in 1949.

A Transformed City: Welcome to the Future

Strasbourg is a thriving, international city that is proud of its multiracial past today. In addition to being a UNESCO World Heritage Site and a center for innovation, it is well-known for its stunning architecture and ability to unite many cultural groups.

Why Choose Strasbourg for Your Next Adventure

The enthralling city of Strasbourg, France, provides a singular fusion of culture, history, and scenic beauty. Just a few of the reasons Strasbourg ought to be your next travel destination are as follows:

1. A Wealthy Past

Strasbourg's history extends back to the Roman era, and it is extensive. Over the ages, the city has been ruled by a number of nations, including the Romans, Germans, and French. The architecture, language, and gastronomy of the city all bear witness to this intriguing legacy.

2. Magnificent Architecture

There are some of France's most exquisite architectural designs in Strasbourg. A UNESCO World Heritage Site, the city's historic core is home to quaint squares, canals, and half-timbered homes.

3. Bright Cultural Life

The city of Strasbourg has a thriving cultural scene. The city is always bustling with festivals, events, and concerts. Theaters and museums abound in Strasbourg as well.

4. Delectable Food

Strasbourg is a gourmet haven. The city is well-known for its authentic Alsatian dishes, such as choucroute (a dish of sauerkraut, pork, and sausages), spätzle (noodles), and flammekueche (a thin pastry with cheese, bacon, and onions).

5. Gorgeous Natural Environment

The Alsace area, where Strasbourg is situated, is renowned for its breathtaking landscapes. The Black Forest in Germany is only a short drive from the city, which is encircled by the Vosges Mountains.

6. An Excellent French Learning Spot

A fantastic location to learn French is Strasbourg. There are several language schools in the city, and you can practice speaking French with locals on a regular basis.

7. A City That Serves All

Everyone may live in Strasbourg. Every age group and interest may find something to see and do. There are lots of parks and playgrounds in the city, which makes it highly family-friendly.

8. A Practical Setting

Strasbourg is situated in a handy area. Traveling to the city by vehicle, train, or airplane is simple. Moreover, Strasbourg is easily accessible by car from other significant European cities including Paris, Frankfurt, and Zurich.

9. A Welcome and Safe City

The city of Strasbourg is friendly and safe. The people in the city are helpful and kind, and there is a low crime rate.

10. The City with Everything

The city of Strasbourg has it all. It is a stunning, lively, and historically significant city with a lot to offer tourists. Strasbourg is the ideal destination for your next journey if you're searching for a city with a distinct charm and a rich cultural history.

CHAPTER 2: PLANNING YOUR JOURNEY

Best Times to Visit Strasbourg

Travelers are drawn to Strasbourg, the charming capital of Alsace, France, by its alluring fusion of culture, history, and delectable cuisine. Although the city is charming all year round, there are specific seasons that provide unique benefits for those looking to have a truly remarkable time in Strasbourg.

Spring: Revealing to the Enchanting Charm of Strasbourg

As Strasbourg emerges from its winter hibernation and takes on the vivid colors of spring, it becomes an enthralling travel destination. Temperatures progressively rise from late March to May, providing comfortable weather for outdoor exploration. Gardens and parks brim with vibrant blossoms, and the city's recognizable half-timbered homes sparkle in the warm rays of the sun.

Summer: Savoring the Celebrations and Outside Getaways

Strasbourg's summertime is a symphony of vibrant festivals and outdoor events. The city comes alive with vitality from June to August, when the streets are filled with lively markets, outdoor concerts, and customary celebrations. Summertime in Strasbourg is a sensory extravaganza, whether you're riding a leisurely bike through the Petite France neighborhood, strolling along the banks of the Ill River, or enjoying outdoor eating in quaint squares.

Fall: An Entire Tapestry of Colors and Calm Ambience

Autumn throws a spell on Strasbourg, as the leaves change into a kaleidoscope of blazing reds, oranges, and yellows. The city has a serene vibe from September to November, which is a pleasant change from the busy summer months. Without the summer crowds, take in the city's museums and historical sites, or explore the Alsace region's charming villages and vineyards outside the city limits.

Winter: An Enchanted Conversion into a Joyful Wonderland

Strasbourg has a mystical makeover as the year comes to an end, covered in sparkling lights and joyous celebration. The city is home to its internationally recognized Christmas markets, which captivate tourists with their alluring scents, traditional handicrafts, and mouthwatering sweets from late November to early December. Take a leisurely stroll through the exquisitely lit streets, savor a comforting glass of vin chaud, and truly embrace the captivating festive atmosphere of the city.

Thoughts for Selecting the Optimal Time to Go

Although Strasbourg has a distinct appeal throughout the year, the best time to visit will rely on your interests and mode of transportation:

For lovers of festivals and the great outdoors: Summer is the best season to take in the city's colorful outdoor events and festivals.

For those interested in art and culture: The months of spring and autumn offer a more sedate environment for visiting museums, historical sites, and art galleries without the throngs of summer visitors.

For those looking for a festive vibe: Winter is the best time to watch Strasbourg magically turn into a wonderland of lights and seasonal cheer, especially during the Christmas season.

Cost-conscious tourists: To save money on lodging and airfare, think about going during the shoulder seasons in the spring (April–May) or fall (September–October).

Guides for Arranging Your Vacation to Strasbourg

In order to guarantee a remarkable trip to Strasbourg, take into account these suggestions:

Make reservations for lodging in advance: Because of its year-round appeal, Strasbourg welcomes tourists, so book your accommodations in advance, especially during the busiest times of the year.

Discover the city by bicycle or on foot: Strasbourg is a great place to explore on foot or by bicycle because of its small size and pedestrian-friendly streets.

Savor the local cuisine: Savor the delectable delicacies of the area, ranging from robust Alsatian fare to delicate French desserts.

Explore beyond the city center: For a taste of true regional charm, explore the Alsace region's charming villages and wineries.

Grab a few French expressions: Basic French language skills will improve your interactions and cultural immersion even though many people know English.

Welcome the unanticipated: Keep an open mind and be prepared to uncover unexpected experiences and hidden jewels in Strasbourg, a city full of surprises.

Navigating Transportation: Getting In and Around

The capital of the Alsace region in eastern France, Strasbourg, has good access to a range of modes of transportation, making it a convenient destination. There are practical and effective ways to get to your destination and take in the city's many attractions, regardless of how you're getting there—by vehicle, rail, or airplane.

Setting Out for Strasbourg

By Aircraft

The main airport serving the city is Strasbourg Entzheim Airport (SXB), which is only 15 kilometers from the city center. The airport has direct flights to several overseas locations as well as major cities in Europe.

Through Train

Being the center of regional and international train services, Strasbourg Train Station is a great choice for visitors arriving from different regions of France, Germany, and Switzerland. The station is in a prime location, close to a lot of hotels and tourist destinations.

In a car

Strasbourg is easily accessible by vehicle thanks to its excellent highway connections. Parking in the city center, however, can be costly and difficult. Think about parking at one of the city's park-and-ride lots or taking public transportation.

How to Navigate Strasbourg

Transportation via Public

Strasbourg's Compagnie des Transports Strasbourgeois (CTS) runs a vast and effective public transport network. The network consists of:

The tram: a system of six tram lines that links the suburbs and rural areas with the city core.

Metro: a system of more than thirty bus lines that serves the whole city and its environs.

Copy: In the heart of the city and at important transportation hubs, taxis are widely accessible.

Tickets for public transport can be bought at machines at bus and tram stops, CTS offices, and certain newsagents.

Additional Modes of Transportation

Strolling: Strasbourg has a pedestrian-friendly center and is a very walkable city.

Cycling: Strasbourg is a fantastic city to explore on a bicycle because to its extensive network of bike paths.

Vessel: Numerous boat cruises that provide an exclusive viewpoint of the city are offered on the Ill River.

A Guide to Using Strasbourg's Transit System

Arrange your travel ahead of time: Make travel plans and schedule checks using the CTS app or website.

Invest in a multi-day pass: If you intend to take public transit frequently, you might want to buy a multi-day pass to save money on fares.

Check your ticket: Before boarding a bus or tram, make sure your ticket is valid.

Be mindful of your surroundings: Pay particular attention to traffic and pedestrians when you're walking or riding a bicycle.

Savor the journey: Utilize Strasbourg's well-functioning transit system to visit the city's numerous sights.

Visa Information and Travel Essentials

For a maximum of ninety days, citizens of Schengen Area countries are exempt from requiring a visa in order to visit Strasbourg. All travelers, though, must have a current passport that is at least three months from the date of anticipated departure, regardless of nationality.

For entry into France, citizens of nations outside the Schengen Area can need a visa. Visa requirements differ according on nationality, therefore it's vital to find out the specifics from the French embassy or consulate in your nation.

Process of Application

The following steps are usually involved in the visa application process:

- Filling out an application for a visa
- Presenting a passport that is currently valid and has enough time left on it
- Providing passport-sized photos for submission
- Presenting evidence of financial capability
- Presenting documentation of travel insurance
- Covering the application expense for a visa

Turnaround Time

The amount of labor at the embassy or consulate and the intricacy of the application determine how long it takes to process a visa application. Generally speaking, you should apply for a visa well in advance of your intended trip.

Essentials for Travel

Poundage

The euro (€) is the currency used in France. Banks, currency exchange bureaus, and certain hotels offer currency exchange services. Although major credit cards are generally accepted, carrying cash on hand is usually a good idea.

Vernacular

French is the official language of France. Although it is spoken in several tourist locations, English is not as common as it is in other European nations. You'll have a better time traveling and interacting with people if you know a few basic French words.

Hospitality

From luxurious hotels to low-cost hostels, Strasbourg has lodging alternatives to fit every budget. It is advised that you reserve your lodging in advance, particularly during popular travel times.

Significance

Type C and E electrical outlets are used in France. You will require an adaptor if you are traveling from a nation where the outlets are different.

Survival Contacts

- Criminal: 17
- Medicine: 15
- Cascade: 18
- Office for Tourists: +33 3 88 75 50 00

Budget-Friendly Accommodations

Strasbourg is a popular tourist destination because of its charming half-timbered homes and lively Christmas markets, but it's also reasonably priced. The following advice can help you locate reasonably priced lodging in Strasbourg:

Think About Remaining in a Hostel

Numerous clean, comfortable hostels in Strasbourg are available at extremely affordable costs. For independent travelers, couples, and groups of friends, hostels are an excellent choice. Several well-liked hostels in Strasbourg are:

Hostel The People - Strasbourg

HI Strasbourg 2 Rives /

Auberge de Jeunesse

Budget of the Strasbourg Center Republic

Discover the Communities Outside the City Center

Staying in an area immediately outside the city center is a good idea because accommodations there are typically more expensive. These communities are frequently well-served by public transportation and provide a more intimate, local feel. Some desirable neighborhoods to take into account are:

- Krugenau
- Neudorf
- Assemblea

Reserve Your Room in Advance

It's generally a good idea to reserve your lodging in advance, especially during popular travel times. This will guarantee that your alternatives are more varied and increase your chances of finding a decent offer.

Take Into Account Other Accommodation Choices

Apart from hostels and hotels, Strasbourg offers a few other less expensive alternatives for lodging. These consist of:

[AirBnb:] A wide range of rooms and apartments in Strasbourg are available for rent on Airbnb.

Surfing on couches: Through the website Couchsurfing, visitors can find residents who are prepared to provide them a free place to stay.

Guides for Cutting Accommodation Costs

Here are some more suggestions for cutting costs on lodging in Strasbourg:

Vacation during the off-season: From November to March, lodging costs are often lower during this time.

Remain midweek: Weekend rates frequently exceed those of weekdays.

Take into account shared accommodations: Share an apartment or room if you are traveling with someone.

Prepare your own food: Cooking your own meals at your apartment or dorm might help you save money as eating out can be costly.

Use public transit to your advantage: In Strasbourg, public transit is reasonably priced and quite effective. Utilize it to navigate the city and reduce the cost of cab rides.

By using these suggestions, you may locate lodgings in Strasbourg that fit your budget and have an enjoyable, reasonably priced vacation to this stunning city.

CHAPTER 3: UNVEILING STRASBOURG'S CHARM

The Strasbourg Experience: Culture and Lifestyle

The intriguing city of Strasbourg, the capital of the Grand Est region in northeastern France, skillfully combines French and German elements to create a distinctive cultural and lifestyle experience. Strasbourg, which is tucked away along the Ill River, has a rich past that is on display in the Grande-Île, a charming maze of half-timbered homes, cobblestone lanes, and attractive canals that is recognized by UNESCO. Beyond its historical appeal, the city has a lot to offer in terms of culture, food, and a relaxed way of life that encourages exploration and leisurely strolls.

Cultural Tapestry: Combining German and French Customs

Strasbourg's important location at the meeting point of Germany and France is reflected in its unique cultural identity. This combination is reflected in the city's architecture, which combines more contemporary German-inspired buildings with half-timbered homes and Gothic churches. Many Strasbourg residents are multilingual, speaking both French and German, demonstrating the blending of cultures even in language.

The calendar of cultural events in the city bears witness to its rich history. Every traveler should see the well-known Strasbourg Christmas Market, a jolly wonderland filled with sparkling lights and alluring scents. Strasbourg holds a number of festivals all year long. The lively Foire de Strasbourg is a customary fair that features cuisine, crafts, and entertainment. The classical Strasbourg Music Festival, on the other hand, features world-class orchestras and soloists.

Culinary Delights: A Culinary Journey

Strasbourg's French and German influences can be found in its symphony of tastes in its food scene. Hearty meals like coq au Riesling, a chicken stew stewed in Alsatian Riesling wine, and choucroute, a flavorful dish based on sauerkraut, are staples of traditional Alsatian cuisine. Savor the kougelhopf, a delicious, buttery yeast cake with a unique crown-like shape that is the city's hallmark dish.

Strasbourg has a number of Michelin-starred restaurants and hip bistros for those looking for a more modern dining experience. Savor the sophisticated flavors at Le Crocodile, try some of the creative dishes at JY's, or take in the lively ambiance of La Cuisine, a busy restaurant serving contemporary French cuisine.

A Relaxed Pace and a Passion for Life Unveiled

The people of Strasbourg have a true appreciation for life's small joys and live at a slow pace. Visitors and cyclists stroll along the city's picturesque streets, and inhabitants congregate in cafés and plazas to mingle and have a leisurely aperitif. The parks and gardens across the city offer peaceful havens that are ideal for getting away from the daily grind.

The people of Strasbourg are proud of their city's environmental awareness and rich cultural legacy. With programs like the Strasbourg Eco-Tram, a zero-emission tram system, and the pedestrian-friendly zones on the Grande-Île, the city is demonstrating its commitment to sustainability.

Exploring Strasbourg: A Vibrant City Journey

The best way to experience Strasbourg's attractions is on foot, as its cobblestone alleys and secret passageways reveal a wealth of charming stores, inviting cafés, and architectural treasures. Take a stroll around the UNESCO-designated World Heritage site, Petite France, and marvel at the half-timbered homes that line the canals. Scale the spire of the Cathédrale Notre-Dame, a magnificent example of Gothic design, to see sweeping city vistas.

Explore Strasbourg's thriving neighborhoods outside of the city center, each with a distinct personality. Discover the chic stores and hip cafés in the Neustadt neighborhood, or take in Krutenau's authentically Alsatian ambience with its quaint half-timbered homes and taverns.

Final Thought: A Soul-Captivating City

Exploring the Historic Districts

Strasbourg's historic districts, each providing a different window into the city's past, vividly maintain the city's rich history. Explore these neighborhoods, which offer architectural treasures, lively cultural activities, and a seductive feeling of nostalgia, from the charming canals of La Petite France to the expansive boulevards of Neustadt.

The Petite France: An Important UNESCO Site

A charming neighborhood that takes you back to the Middle Ages is called La Petite France, or "Little France," and it is located on the Grande-Île, a UNESCO World Heritage Site. There is a certain allure to its winding, little alleyways that are dotted with half-timbered homes from the 16th and 17th centuries. Once humming with activity, the district's tanneries, mills, and fishermen's cottages are now lovely memories of Strasbourg's history.

Admire the half-timbered houses' colorful façade, delicate wooden beams, and geranium-adorned windows as you meander around the cobblestone streets. Wander over the covered bridges, which were originally used to shield traders and their goods from the weather, and spend some time admiring how the half-timbered homes reflected in the canals.

Grande-Île: Strasbourg's Central Area

Strasbourg's historic core, the Grande-Île, is a maze of quaint streets, stunning buildings, and enthralling squares. The Cathédrale Notre-Dame, a Gothic masterpiece that has served as the city's emblem for centuries, is located at its center. Visitors are in awe of its astronomical clock, elaborate stained glass windows, and towering façade made of pink sandstone.

Discover the cathedral's surrounding small streets, which are dotted with eateries, cafés, and stores. Explore the 16th-century half-timbered Maison Kammerzell, which features murals in the Renaissance style, and take in the splendor of the Palais Rohan, which used to be the Prince-Bishops of Strasbourg's palace.

Neustadt: A Combination of French and German Elements

The ancient attractions of the Grande-Île are dramatically contrasted with the Neustadt neighborhood, which was constructed during German authority in the late 19th century, across the Ill River. Its broad boulevards, which are bordered by imposing buildings and great boulevards, showcase the era's architectural designs.

See the Place de la République, a large plaza with a colossal fountain and towering structures all around, including the Palais du Rhin, which served as the German government's old seat. Discover the lively streets of the Neustadt, home to chic shops, welcoming cafés, and fine dining establishments serving a diverse audience.

Krutenau: A Flavor of Traditional Alsace

The Krutenau neighborhood, which is outside the city center, provides a window into Strasbourg's Alsatian past. Its winding streets are full of character, with half-timbered cottages along them and flower boxes hanging from them. Explore classic Alsatian eateries that offer filling fare like coq au

Riesling and choucroute, and indulge in the tastes of the area's well-known wines.

See the beautifully preserved interior of the Église Saint-Nicolas, a 12th-century Romanesque church. Discover the artisanal products, fresh food, and Alsatian delights offered by local vendors at the Krutenau market.

Must-Try Local Cuisine and Dining Hotspots

The region's rich history and cultural legacy are reflected in the seamless fusion of French and German elements seen in Alsace's cuisine. The cuisine of Alsace is characterized by its use of robust, savory recipes that frequently feature regional items such as potatoes, sauerkraut, and pig.

1. Choucroute: An Icon of Cuisine

The classic Alsatian cuisine is choucroute, a flavorful stew made with sauerkraut and a variety of meats, including duck, geese, and pork. The dish's rich and filling heartiness is provided by the meats, while the acidic and sour flavor comes from the fermented cabbage, or sauerkraut. Choucroute is typically served with a side of mustard and potatoes.

2. A Culinary Delight: Coq au Riesling

Another traditional Alsatian cuisine is coq au Riesling, which is chicken stew cooked in Alsatian Riesling wine. The chicken gains layers of flavor from the classic spices like juniper berries, bay leaves, and thyme, as well as a subtle sweetness and acidity from the Riesling. Traditionally, potatoes or spaetzle—a kind of egg noodle—are served with coq au Riesling.

3. Baeckeoffe: A Filling and Tasty Soup

Traditional Alsatian stew baeckeoffe is cooked in a deep pot that is sealed with dough and layers of meat, potatoes, and veggies. A rich and flavorful dish is produced by allowing the flavors to blend over a slow cooking period. Spaetzle or rice is frequently served alongside bain geoffe.

4. A Tart with Savory Toppings, Flammekueche

Tarte flambée, or flammekueche, is a thin-crust pizza topped with cheese, bacon, onions, and crème fraîche, among other delicious ingredients. The tart's crispy crust and smoky flavor come from cooking it in a wood-fired oven. Flammekueche is frequently used as an appetizer or snack.

5. Spätzle: An Adaptable Noodle for Egg

Egg noodles, or spätzle, are a common element in Alsatian cooking. It can be eaten as a main course with a variety of sauces or toppings, or it is frequently served as a side dish with robust stews like choucroute or baeckeoffe.

Eating Destinations

Enjoying the Gastronomic Treasures of Alsace

There are restaurants in Strasbourg to suit every taste and price, making for a lively eating scene. Here are some suggestions for tasting the finest food that Alsace has to offer:

1. A Culinary Tradition at La Maison Kammerzell

Housed in a half-timbered building from the 16th century, La Maison Kammerzell is a historic restaurant in the center of La Petite France. The eatery offers classic Alsatian fare in a quaint and genuine setting.

2. Le Tire-Bouchon: A Preferred Location

A well-liked local landmark, Le Tire-Bouchon is renowned for its real Alsatian food and vibrant ambiance. A large assortment of classic meals, such as baeckeoffe, coq au Riesling, and choucroute, are available at the restaurant.

3. Au Crocodile: An Experience with a Michelin Star

A sophisticated and creative perspective on Alsatian food may be found at the Michelin-starred Au Crocodile restaurant. Chef Frédéric Anton uses contemporary methods to produce recipes that highlight the fresh, in-season ingredients from the area.

4. La Cuisine: A Contemporary Bistro in Alsace

Fresh, in-season ingredients are the main feature of the modern Alsatian cuisine served at La Cuisine, a lively cafe. The cuisine at the restaurant is always changing to showcase the chef's inventiveness and love of regional ingredients.

5. Les Secrets d'Aphrodite: A Heavenly Place for Wine Lovers

The quaint wine bar and restaurant Les Secrets d'Aphrodite is well-known for its wide assortment of Alsatian wines. Additionally, the restaurant has a selection of tapas and small appetizers that go well with wine.

Embracing the Strasbourg Lifestyle

Strasbourg offers a distinctive lifestyle that is both refined and charming due to its unique blend of French and German influences. Here's a guide to enjoying Strasbourg's distinct charm and embracing its lifestyle, whether you're a short-term visitor or looking to become fully immersed in the community.

1. Adopt a Cycling Philosophy

With an extensive network of cycling routes that make exploring the city simple, Strasbourg is a cyclist's dream come true. Get on a bike and explore the city's hidden treasures, such the lively neighborhoods of Neustadt and the picturesque canals of La Petite France, without having to drive. Riding two wheels around the city's lovely streets, you can join the residents and take in the relaxed pace of life.

2. Savor the Cuisine of Alsace

Alsace offers a rich and varied gourmet experience thanks to its culinary traditions, which harmoniously combine German and French influences. Savor the region's specialties, which include the filling choucroute, the luscious coq au Riesling, and the cozy baeckeoffe, slowly. Enjoy a glass of locally produced Alsatian wine with your lunch. This wine is known for its perfect balance of acidity and sweetness.

3. Take in the Culture's Delights

Strasbourg is a center of culture, with exciting theaters, prestigious museums, and a thriving arts scene. Take in a performance at the Opéra National du Rhin, tour the Musée des

Beaux-Arts, or visit the breathtaking Cathédrale Notre-Dame to fully immerse yourself in the city's rich cultural tapestry.

4. Visit the Markets and Fairs Around the City

Markets and festivals in Strasbourg are a veritable gold mine of regional goods, handmade crafts, and quintessential Alsatian fare. Explore the stalls of the bustling Marché Bastille, a farmers' market that takes place every Saturday morning, or take a leisurely stroll through the Marché de Noël, a mystical Christmas market filled with enchanting scents and sparkling lights.

5. Adopt a Relaxed Tempo

The people of Strasbourg have a true appreciation for life's small joys and live at a slow pace. Enjoy a leisurely aperitif at a sidewalk café, a leisurely stroll along the Ill River, or some sun exposure in one of the city's many parks. Savor the time and accept the slower tempo.

6. Uncover the Distinctive Charm of the Neighborhoods

Explore Strasbourg's varied neighborhoods, each with an own personality, by venturing outside the city center. Explore the half-timbered homes and classic Alsatian pubs in Krutenau, or take a break from it all at the chic cafés and fashionable boutiques of Neustadt. Both neighborhoods have cobblestone streets.

7. Accept the Sustainability Initiatives of the City

With programs like the Strasbourg Eco-Tram, a zero-emission tram system, and the pedestrian-friendly zones in the Grande-Île, Strasbourg is a leader in sustainability. Participate in the city's environmentally conscious initiatives by reducing waste, patronizing neighborhood businesses, and selecting eco-friendly modes of transportation.

8. Establish Contact with Locals

Talk to the amiable residents and engage in discussion. Speak French or German, and don't be shy about seeking advice on must-try activities or hidden treasures. You will gain a greater understanding of the culture and character of the city by hearing the perspectives of the residents.

9. Adopt a Joyful Attitude

Strasbourg's thriving cultural sector is reflected in the multitude of festivals held there every year. Take in the vibrant atmosphere of the Foire de Strasbourg, the festive atmosphere of the Strasbourg Christmas Market, or the classical music of the Strasbourg Music Festival.

10. Cherish the Small Joys

Enjoy the little things in life that Strasbourg has to offer. Savor a leisurely breakfast at a neighborhood café, have a picnic in the Parc de l'Orangerie, or just meander through the quaint streets of the city to take in the allure of the place.

CHAPTER 4: TOP ATTRACTIONS AND LANDMARKS

Strasbourg Cathedral: A Gothic Masterpiece

The Cathedral of Notre Dame de Strasbourg, a magnificent example of Gothic architecture, towers majestically over the center of Strasbourg, France. With a height of 465 feet (142 meters), its beautiful spire has long served as a representation of the city's illustrious past and resilient character. Built between the twelfth and fifteenth centuries, the cathedral is a magnificent example of the craftsmanship and ability of the medieval builders, and its magnificent size and minute features have mesmerized tourists for generations.

A Trip Across Time

The majesty of the cathedral is immediately apparent as one enters its dimly lighted interior. Elevated vaults, intricately carved stonework, and glittering stained glass windows evoke a feeling of spiritual devotion and ethereal beauty. The delicate decorations of the triforium and clerestory galleries enhance the impression of verticality and light within the cathedral's wide nave, which rises to a height of 32 meters (104 feet). The cathedral is a marvel of engineering.

Architectural Magnificence

The cathedral's magnificent west façade, designed in a flamboyant Gothic style, is unquestionably its most remarkable feature. The façade, embellished with an abundance of sculptures, gargoyles, and filigree tracery, is a magnificent treat for the eyes. The cathedral's inner sanctum can be accessed through the magnificent central portal, which is flanked by imposing statues and framed by beautiful decorations.

A Priceless Art and Historical Relic

The cathedral is home to a multitude of artwork and historical artifacts in addition to its stunning architecture. The 16th-century mechanical marvel known as the Astronomical Clock captivates audiences with its daily exhibition of animated figures and celestial displays. Numerous bishops and other dignitaries' remains are kept in the crypt of the cathedral, which also features a masterpiece of Renaissance craftsmanship in its choir with its beautifully carved seats and stained glass windows.

A Sign of the Identity of Strasbourg

Strasbourg Cathedral is more than just a place of worship; with its lofty spire and intricate architectural elements, it is a representation of the city's character and a living reminder of its rich history. The cathedral has been a source of inspiration and optimism for ages, and its presence has shaped the skyline and character of the city. Currently recognized as a UNESCO World Heritage Site, the cathedral attracts tourists from all over the world who come to admire its splendor and learn about its extensive past.

A Guide to Touring the Strasbourg Cathedral

Plan your visit during the day, when sunshine illuminates the stained glass windows and casts a pleasant glow on the interior, to fully appreciate the majesty of the cathedral. Give yourself plenty of time to tour the cathedral's many chapels, take in the finely detailed sculptures, and climb the tower for sweeping city views. If you want a fully immersive experience, think about going to a service or concert in the cathedral's sacred halls.

La Petite France: A Picturesque Canal District

Located in the center of Strasbourg, France, La Petite France is a picturesque canal neighborhood that perfectly captures the allure of the city. The district's name, which translates to "Little France," accurately captures the charming ambiance of a village from a fairy tale. The neighborhood is made up of meandering cobblestone alleys that are dotted with half-timbered houses, reflecting the vibrant façade of these buildings in the serene canals that meander through it.

The history of La Petite France dates back to the Middle Ages, when it was a thriving center for tanners and millers. Numerous half-timbered homes in the neighborhood date back to the 16th and 17th centuries, demonstrating the district's rich historical legacy through its maintained architecture.

The district's whimsical charm is enhanced by these charming structures, which include colorful accents and delicate wooden beams.

The district's signature feature, the canals, give the surroundings a serene quality. Gondolier-style boats are a unique opportunity for visitors to take in the stunning surroundings as they glide over the canals with grace. The two sides of the canals are linked by charming bridges that are decorated with flowers and other vegetation, beckoning people to wander along their banks and take in the peaceful ambiance.

The Maison des Tanneurs, a 16th-century tannery that now houses a traditional Alsatian restaurant, and the Maison des Ponts Couverts, a medieval bridge with covered passageways that provide picturesque views of the canals, are two hidden gems that can be found amidst the maze-like streets and canals.

La Petite France is a treasure trove for art lovers, with a plethora of galleries and antique stores exhibiting regional treasures and craftsmanship. You are likely to find something that speaks to you, whether it be exquisite wood carvings, delicate hand-painted pottery, or distinctive jewelry.

La Petite France is transformed into a mystical world as the sun sets. Enchantment and romance are created by the mellow glow of lanterns casting a warm, inviting light on the half-timbered houses and cobblestone streets.

La Petite France offers an incredible experience that will leave you fascinated and itching to return, whether your goals are to take a leisurely stroll along the canals, have a romantic supper by the water's edge, or have the opportunity to immerse yourself in the district's rich history and artistic culture.

The Strasbourg Museum Trail

Discover the rich history, artwork, and cultural legacy of Strasbourg through the fascinating Strasbourg Museum Trail. This route passes through a wide range of museums, each providing a distinctive window into various aspects of Strasbourg's history and current state of affairs. This is a thorough reference to the well-known museums along the route:

Strasbourg Museum Path

1. Musée des Beaux-Arts (Strasburg Museum of Fine Arts): This museum, which is housed in a magnificent 18th-century structure, has an extraordinary collection of European decorative arts, paintings, and sculptures that date from the Middle Ages to the 19th century. Work by well-known artists including Goya,

Rubens, and Botticelli is on display for visitors to admire.

2. The Museum of Alsace (Musée Alsacien): Visit this lovely museum to fully immerse yourself in Alsatian customs and culture. It provides insight into the agricultural heritage of the area by showcasing crafts, furniture, folk art, and traditional costumes.

3. The Strasbourg Historical Museum (Musée Historique de Strasbourg): Explore the past of Strasbourg by visiting this museum, which is located in a former slaughterhouse. It showcases the evolution of the city over time, with exhibits on daily life, politics, and the economy spanning from the medieval to the modern era.

4. The Museum of Modern and Contemporary Art (Musée d'Art Moderne et Contemporain): This is a must-visit museum for fans of modern art. It displays a wide range of modern artworks from both domestic and foreign artists, such as paintings, sculptures, installations, and multimedia shows.

5. **Tomi Ungerer Museum** : This museum, which honors the renowned novelist and illustrator Tomi Ungerer, features his wacky and provocative creations, including satirical artwork, children's books, and illustrations.

6. **Museum of Zoology (Musée Zoologique):** This museum, which is great for those who enjoy the outdoors, has a large collection of skeletons, interactive exhibits, and taxidermied animals that provide visitors an understanding of global biodiversity and animal species.

7. **The Prints and Drawings Gallery, or Cabinet des Estampes et des Dessins:** This gallery is a haven for artists, with a vast

collection of prints, drawings, and etchings that provide a window into the development of graphic arts across time.

8. Strasbourg's Historical Museum (Musée de la Ville de Strasbourg): Discover the history and evolution of Strasbourg by delving into a wide array of relics, records, and interactive exhibits that illuminate the city's rich architectural, social, and cultural legacy.

Advice for Visitors

Ticket Options: If you want to visit several museums at a lower price, think about getting a museum pass.
Guided Tours: A lot of museums provide multilingual guided tours that offer a greater understanding of the displays.
Hours of Operation and Holidays: Prior to scheduling your visit, find out each museum's

opening times and any possible holiday closures.

Meeting Point: Wheelchair accessibility is available in most museums, however it's best to check beforehand for special accessibility features.

Through the intriguing and enriching Strasbourg Museum Trail, visitors may get a deeper appreciation for the city's art, history, and traditions while exploring its colorful cultural tapestry.

Riverside Parks and Gardens

The city of Strasbourg, which is tucked away on the banks of the Ill River, is home to an amazing system of riverbank parks and gardens that provide peaceful havens among the busy streets. Both locals and tourists may unwind, have fun, and establish a relationship with nature in these lush havens.

Jardin des Deux Rives: An Icon of Friendship Across Borders

The Jardin des Deux Rives, which spans the Ill River between Germany and France, is a representation of friendship and collaboration beyond national boundaries. Since its opening in 2004, this vast park has blended natural with urban design through a variety of plants, trees, and pathways.

Wander through the park's serene meadows, have a picnic beneath the shady canopy of tall trees, or take in the vivid blooms in the flowerbeds. Throughout the year, the park also holds a range of activities, such as cultural festivals and outdoor concerts.

Parc de l'Orangerie: A Calm Haven with a Touch of History

Founded in the 17th century, the Park de l'Orangerie has a timeless appeal and elegance. Its well-kept lawns, scattered with fountains and statues, offer plenty of room for calm walks or introspective times.

Parc de l'Étoile: Quiet Shores and sweeping views

Perched on the banks of the Ill River, the Parc de l'Étoile provides a panoramic perspective of the cityscape. Its gently sloping, lushly vegetated hills offer a tranquil haven from the busy city core.

Wander along the park's meandering trails on a bike or stroll, relax on one of the many benches that provide river views, or visit the remains of the Étoile Fort, which dates back to the fourteenth century.

The Jardin Botanique de Strasbourg: A Sanctuary for Botanists

Plant lovers will find paradise at the Jardin Botanique de Strasbourg, which features an extensive variety of plants from all over the world. Its carefully kept greenhouses, arboretum, and gardens offer an enthralling tour of the plant life.

In the apothecary garden, guests can discover the therapeutic qualities of herbs, wonder at the exotic plants in the tropical greenhouse, or take in the vivid hues of the rose garden.

Strasbourg's Suspendus Gardens: An Upright Sanctuary

A vertical respite in the middle of the city's metropolitan landscape is provided by the remarkable architectural wonder that is the Jardins Suspendus de Strasbourg. These rooftop gardens offer a peaceful haven with a bird's-eye perspective of the surrounding cityscape, all situated atop a former parking lot.

Wander around the gardens' meandering walks, unwind under the pergolas' shade, or have dinner in the restaurant with its expansive views.

These riverbank parks and gardens, each with its own unique personality and allure, are vital green areas in the thriving city of Strasbourg. They give locals and guests the chance to relax from the daily grind, re-connect with nature, and take in the beauty of the natural world. The parks and gardens along the river in Strasbourg provide something for everyone, whether they are looking for a calm getaway, a peaceful picnic area, or an instructive botanical experience.

CHAPTER 5: INSIDER TIPS FOR A MEMORABLE JOURNEY

Local Experts' Insights

Go beyond the well-traveled tourist routes and embrace the spirit of exploration as you set off on your adventure around Strasbourg. Try these insider suggestions from residents who are familiar with Strasbourg like the back of their hands if you want to fully immerse yourself in the lively culture of the city and discover its hidden treasures.

1. Experience La Petite France's Charm

Take a stroll through La Petite France, a charming canal district with an enduring allure. Stroll down the cobblestone streets that are bordered by half-timbered houses and brightly colored flora. Enjoy a leisurely boat trip along the canals to fully appreciate Strasbourg's natural beauty while taking in the enchanted ambiance.

2. Savor the Flavors of Alsatian Cuisine

Savor the delicious cuisine of Alsace as you go on a culinary adventure there. Try the flammekueche, a crispy, thin pizza with bacon, onions, and crème fraîche on top. Savor the flavorful choucroute, a filling dish made with fermented cabbage, pork, and potatoes. Enjoy a slice of the delicious kougelhopf, a typical Alsatian cake with a distinctive ring-shaped mold, while you have the chance.

3. Take a Festive Cheerful Tour of the Christmas Markets

Strasbourg turns into a mystical wonderland during the holidays, attracting tourists from all over the world with its enchanted Christmas markets. Explore the enchanting ambiance filled with festivity and shimmering lights. Enjoy the delicious delicacies and handcrafted presents while indulging in the smells of mulled wine and gingerbread.

4. Come to Strasbourg's Cafes and Bars and Feel the Local Spirit

Go to the vibrant bars and quaint cafés in Strasbourg to get a sense of the local vibe. Start a discussion with the locals; they would be happy to offer their insights and insider knowledge about the area. Savor a croissant and café au lait for a leisurely morning, or relax in a classic Alsatian bar with a cold glass of regional beer.

5. Explore Outside the City Core: Day Trips and Adjacent Treasures

The splendor of Strasbourg is not limited to the downtown area. Take a day excursion to the charming village of Obernai, which is home to vineyards and half-timbered homes. See the magnificent Haut-Koenigsbourg Castle, a historic stronghold atop a hill with stunning views of the surrounding landscape.

6. Adopt Eco-Friendly Decisions and Sustainable Practices

Travelers who care about the environment should definitely visit Strasbourg because of its dedication to sustainability. The public transit system is a convenient and ample option. Take a stroll or a bike ride around the city to take in the fresh air and relaxed pace. Savoring seasonal, fresh vegetables and handcrafted goods will help you support neighborhood businesses and markets.

7. Accept the Unexpected: Coincidence and Novel Findings

While you tour Strasbourg, give yourself permission to be taken aback and to welcome the unexpected. Explore paths less traveled and you'll come across undiscovered treasures nestled in peaceful nooks. Talk to locals; they are willing to share their experiences and viewpoints. Allow serendipity to lead you to memorable events and unanticipated meetings.

8. Indulge and Establish Connections: Savor the Slow Travel Experience

Avoid the urge to visit Strasbourg's attractions quickly. Rather, adopt the slow trip approach and give oneself the opportunity to fully absorb the beat and ambiance of the city. Spend some time in a café, taking in the lively conversation of the patrons and the smells of freshly brewed coffee. Take a stroll through the parks and take in the peace and beauty of the natural world.

9. Seize the Moment: A Photographer's Dream Come True

Strasbourg is a photographer's dream come true, with an abundance of interesting subjects to photograph. Seize the tranquil reflections in the canals, the vivid colors of the Christmas markets, or the majesty of the Gothic church. Using your lens, uncover surprising details and hidden nooks to showcase the city's distinct personality.

Hidden Gems: Off the Beaten Path

Strasbourg has a wealth of undiscovered beauties that are just waiting to be found, hidden away behind the well-known buildings and tourist destinations. For those who explore beyond the well-traveled roads, these off-the-beaten-path discoveries offer a glimpse into the city's rich history, vibrant culture, and local charm, making for a genuinely immersive experience.

1. Here at Le Vaisseau: Visit Le Vaisseau, a special museum created for kids and families, to immerse yourself in a world of science and discovery. Discover hands-on displays that pique your interest and promote exploration, ranging from exploring the secrets of the human body to manipulating light and music.

2. The Museum Tomi Ungerer: Explore the wacky and provocative world of renowned Alsatian novelist and illustrator Tomi Ungerer. His caustic humor and social commentary are displayed in a vast collection of his paintings, sculptures, and sketches held by the museum.

3. Saint-Pierre-le-Jeune Church: Enter the calm and venerable Église Saint-Pierre-le-Jeune, an 11th-century Romanesque church. Admire its elaborate design, which includes the imposing Romanesque portal and the cloister's remnants.

4. Vauban Barrage: Discover the Barrage Vauban, a 17th-century dam that protected Strasbourg strategically. Take in the expansive views of the city and the surrounding countryside as you stroll along the pedestrian walkway built across the dam.

5. Intimidation: Experience the cutting edge of modern art at Stimultania, a nonprofit organization that supports experimental projects and up-and-coming artists. Explore cutting-edge performances, workshops, and exhibitions that will inspire and challenge you.

6. Historical Cave of Strasbourg's Civil Hospices: Explore the historic cellar of the 14th-century Cave historique des hospices civils de Strasbourg and go on a subterranean adventure. Discover the intricate passageways adorned with numerous wine bottles and gain insight into the abundant wine-making customs of the area.

7. The Tanneurs' Mansion: Visit the Maison des Tanneurs, a museum that was once a 16th-century tannery, to learn about the history of leatherworking. Admire the architecture of the restored building while exploring the exhibits that highlight the equipment and methods used in the traditional tanning process.

8. Ponts Couverts Maison: Wander along the Pont du Corbeau, also called the Pont Neuf, and stop to see the quaint Maison des Ponts Couverts, a covered passageway from the Middle Ages. Savor the stunning views of the nearby cityscape and the Ill River.

9. The Garden of Deux Rives: Relax in the peaceful Jardin des Deux Rives, a park that spans the Ill River on both the German and French banks. Take in the expansive vistas of the city skyline as you stroll along the well-kept lawns scattered with fountains and statues.

10. The Suspendus Garden of Strasbourg: Get away from the bustle of the city and head up to the Jardins Suspendus de Strasbourg, which are rooftop gardens built on an old parking lot. Savor a meal at the restaurant with its panoramic views, unwind among the lush foliage, and take in the unique viewpoint of the town.

Go off the beaten track and let these undiscovered beauties lead you to Strasbourg's hidden secrets as you explore areas not often visited. Immerse yourself in the true spirit of Strasbourg with these off-the-beaten-path discoveries, which offer a singular and engaging experience ranging from peaceful gardens and fascinating museums to historical landmarks and modern art venues.

Cultural Etiquette and Traditions

Strasbourg is a vibrant city with a rich cultural history that combines German and French influences to create a distinctive fusion of traditions and customs. Understanding these customs and etiquette rules will help you to fully enjoy the city's charm and respect the local way of life.

Hello and Etiquette

Greetings: The traditional way to welcome someone is with a handshake. For informal meetings, a simple "bonjour" or "bonsoir" (good evening) is appropriate. Use "Madame" or "Monsieur" in more formal contexts, and then the person's last name.

Courtesies and Respect: In Strasbourg, courtesies are highly regarded. Say things like "merci" (thank you) and "s'il vous plaît" (please) a lot. Show consideration and decency to those in positions of authority and elders.

Seating Manners

Table manners: Keep your elbows off the table, sit up straight, and preserve proper posture. When dining, make sure to cut your food with a knife and fork and to use clean utensils. Also, try not to make too much noise.

Bread Etiquette: An essential component of Alsatian cooking is bread. It is usual not to cut bread with a knife, but to break off small pieces with your hands.

Tipping: Although it's not as demanded as in some other nations, tipping is traditional in restaurants. Generally speaking, a modest gratuity of five to ten percent of the whole price is adequate.

Traditions and Customs in the Area

Christmas Markets: Travelers from all over the world go to Strasbourg for its well-known Christmas markets. Savor classic Alsatian fare, take in the joyful mood, and take in the alluring setting.

La Petite France: Take a stroll through this lovely canal region, which features quaint bridges and half-timbered homes. Savor a leisurely boat trip along the canals, take in the serene ambiance, and see the architectural grandeur.

Strasbourg Cathedral: Take a tour of this magnificent example of Gothic architecture, the Strasbourg Cathedral. Take in the exquisite workmanship, be in awe of the stained glass windows, and ascend the tower for sweeping city vistas.

Events & Festivities

Strasbourg Wine Festival: Experience the lively atmosphere and sample some of the region's finest wines by attending this annual July festival.

Festival de la Chanson Française: Attend this lively celebration of French chanson and lose yourself in the sounds of French music.

Festival d'Automne: Take in a wide range of modern dance, theater, and music performances at this multifaceted arts festival.

Communication and Language

French and German: In Strasbourg, people speak both French and German quite frequently. Although it's helpful to know a few simple French words, feel free to speak English as many people in the area are multilingual.

Nonverbal Communication: When speaking, make eye contact; this is regarded as a respectful gesture. A friendly gesture such as a handshake is customary, but a light tap on the arm can also be used to express warmth.

Honoring Regional Values

Environmental Awareness: Sustainability is a top priority for Strasbourg. Use public transit, reduce your waste, and patronize environmentally conscious companies as a way to show your support for the city's efforts.

Respect for Diversity: Strasbourg is proud of its diverse history. Be welcoming, accepting, and tolerant of the city's variety.

Preserving Cultural Heritage: The rich history and customs of Strasbourg are highly valued. By enjoying the city's sights, local customs, and cultural institutions, you may show respect for the city's cultural legacy.

Comprehending and honoring Strasbourg's customs and cultural etiquette will improve your trip, help you make connections with the locals, and make a good impression on them as a guest.

Maximizing Your Experience on a Budget

Traveling to Strasbourg, a fascinating city with a rich cultural history, doesn't have to be costly. You may take advantage of the city's many attractions, sample its delectable cuisine, and take in its lively environment without going over budget if you put a little thought and effort into arranging ahead.

1. Adopt the Use of Public Transportation

With trams, buses, and boats among its many modes of public transportation, Strasbourg has an excellent system. Choose these cost-effective and practical ways to get around the city to avoid paying for expensive taxi rides or rental cars.

2. Find Free Things to Do

The magnificent Strasbourg Cathedral, the charming La Petite France neighborhood, and the tranquil Jardin des Deux Rives park are just a few of the city's most well-known attractions that are open for free entry. Utilize these free treasures to fully immerse yourself in the history and beauty of the city.

3. Check Out the Local Cafes and Market

Visit authentic Alsatian markets and cafes to delve deeper into the local cuisine and go beyond the tourist traps. Try some of the more reasonably priced regional specialties, such as flammekueche, choucroute, and kougelhopf.

4. Make Use of Accommodation Choices

Strasbourg has a range of lodging choices to fit different price ranges. Instead of spending a fortune on hotels, think about booking accommodations at hostels, guesthouses, or Airbnbs, which frequently offer a more genuine and local experience.

5. Carry Light and Cleverly

By bringing minimal belongings, you can avoid paying for excess baggage and effortlessly move around the city on foot or using public transport. Take into account the weather and the activities you have scheduled when selecting your clothing.

6. Benefit from Off-Season Prices

If possible, try visiting Strasbourg in the off-season, which is usually from November to March, when costs for lodging, airfare, and tourists are often lower.

Make Use of Complementary Walking Tours

Take one of the free walking tours led by knowledgeable locals to learn about the history, sites, and undiscovered attractions of the city. These tours offer insightful commentary and suggestions from local experts.

8. Accept the Visual Arts

There are a lot of museums and art galleries in Strasbourg, and a lot of them provide free entry on certain days or nights. Take in the bustling art culture of the city without having to shell out a lot of money for admission.

9. Look for Local Advice

Never be afraid to seek locals for advice on good deals on dining establishments, undiscovered treasures, and inexpensive things to do. Their knowledge may help you find genuine, one-of-a-kind experiences that you might not have found on your own.

10. Adopt A Slow Pace

Avoid the temptation to visit Strasbourg's attractions quickly. Rather, adopt the slow trip mindset and relish every second. Spend less money and make lasting memories by hanging out in cafes, strolling through parks, and experiencing the local way of life.

Recall that saving money on travel doesn't have to mean sacrificing quality. Through the adoption of regional traditions, discovery of undiscovered treasures, and utilization of cost-effective choices, you can really savor

Strasbourg's allure and make priceless memories...

CHAPTER 6: DAY TRIPS AND BEYOND

Excursions to Nearby Villages

Beyond Strasbourg's enthralling avenues and famous sites, the Alsace area reveals a tapestry of charming villages, each with its own distinct personality and allure. Set off on an exciting day excursion and explore the vineyards and undulating hills that characterize this stunning area. Experience the mouthwatering cuisine, lively culture, and extensive history of these enchanting locations.

Riquewihr: A Village from a Fairy Tale Freezed in Time

Enter the charming village of Riquewihr, where it seems as though time has stopped. This medieval jewel, tucked away among vineyards, features half-timbered cottages with flower-adorned exteriors, cobblestone alleys, and quaint squares. Walk along the main avenue, the Rue du Général de Gaulle, which is flanked by quaint cafcs, stores, and wineries. Admire the Dolder Tower, a 13th-century reminder of the village's defenses. Explore the rich history of the community at the House of the Coopers and pay homage to the renowned Alsatian artist's creations at the Hansi Museum. Savor the flavors of the Alsatian region by indulging in a typical lunch at one of the neighborhood restaurants.

Kaysersberg: A Royal Past Embracing a Medieval Gem

Travel to Kaysersberg, a hamlet steeped in medieval history, where the majestic Château de Kaysersberg stands as the village's crown. Stroll down the charming streets that are bordered by vibrant half-timbered homes that are decorated with bougainvillea and geraniums. Discover the Fortified Bridge from the 13th century, which bears witness to the village's defensive history. See the Town Hall, a Renaissance masterpiece with murals that illustrate myths from the area. Climb the narrow lanes to the 13th-century stronghold known as Château de Kaysersberg, which provides stunning views of the valleys and vineyards around it.

Eguisheim: The Origin of Charm and Wine

Take a day trip to Eguisheim, a quaint community known for being the origin of Alsace's Grand Cru wines, which is tucked away among vineyards. Wander around the narrow alleyways that are dotted with half-timbered homes that have balconies full of flowers. Discover the ruins of the village's medieval defenses—its three gates. See the 12th-century Château du Haut-Koenigsbourg, which is situated atop a hill with a view of the vineyards and village below. Climb the Dagsberg Tower, a watchtower from the 13th century that provides expansive views of the surrounding landscape. Savor the well-known Alsatian wines by partaking in a wine tasting at one of the many vineyards in the village.

Mittelbergheim: A Eternal Village of Partial-Timbered Magnificence

Visit Mittelbergheim, a charming community tucked away at the base of Mont Sainte-Odile. Take in the beautifully restored half-timbered homes that are accented with vibrant flower displays. Visit the 13th-century Fortified

Church of Saint-Pierre-et-Paul to learn about the village's medieval history. Explore the Winzerhof, a Renaissance manor house turned museum highlighting the history of winemaking in the village. Take a stroll among the nearby vineyards and lose yourself in the peaceful splendor of the Alsatian countryside.

Châteaut-Königsbourg Castle: An Elegant Stronghold Perched Above the Hills

Reach the summit of the Vosges Mountains to explore the magnificent Haut-Kœnigsbourg Castle, a castle from the 12th century that sits atop a hill with a view of the Alsace area. Imagine the castle's involvement in mediaeval conflicts and sieges as you explore its majestic ramparts, towers, and courtyards. Take in the opulent interiors of the castle, which are furnished with antique furniture, armor, and tapestries. Visit the museum to learn about the rich history of the castle and the lives of those who inhabited it, as well as its strategic significance. Climb the towers of the castle to get a beautiful overview over the neighboring villages, woodlands, and vineyards.

A Guide to Organizing Your Trips

Rent a car: Take advantage of the flexibility and freedom to see the area at your own speed.

Make your travel plan: Select the villages that most appeal to you and take the distance between them into account.

Allocate enough time for investigation: Every village is worthy of a slow walk and some time to appreciate its own special charm.

Embrace local experiences: To fully immerse yourself in the culture and food of the area, visit local markets, wineries, and cafés.

Always dress in accordance with the weather: carry an umbrella in case of sudden downpours.

Delight in the voyage: Bask in the views, relish the cuisine, and lose yourself in the captivating ambiance of the

Wine Tasting in the Alsace Region

France's Alsace region is well known for its charming villages, undulating hills, and vineyards. Beyond its breathtaking landscape, Alsace is a wine lover's paradise, providing a singular and wonderful wine tasting experience. Alsace has a long history of winemaking that dates back to the Roman era. As a result, the region produces a wide variety of wines, from exquisite and nuanced reds to crisp and refreshing whites.

A Tour of the Wine Route in Alsace

Set out on an adventure along the 170-kilometer Alsace Wine Route, which meanders through the center of the region's vineyards. Explore the world of Alsatian wine and discover quaint villages, historic wineries, and stunning views.

A Harmony of Wines from Alsace

The characteristic white wines of Alsace, including Sylvaner, Riesling, Gewürztraminer, and Pinot Gris, are highly appreciated for their well-balanced sweetness, crisp acidity, and rich perfume. The rich food of the area, which includes filling salads, creamy cheeses, and robust meat dishes, goes well with these wines.

Alsace is also known for its exquisite red wines, mostly made from Pinot Noir grapes, which are a more robust option for wine lovers. These wines have a lovely harmony of subtle tannins, hints of spice, and rich fruit flavors.

Comprehensive Wine Tasting Events

The wineries in Alsace provide a range of wine sampling options to suit every preference and price range. You will be able to experience the rich history of winemaking in the area, discover the various grape varieties, and appreciate the mouthwatering flavors of Alsatian wines through everything from private cellar visits to big dégustations.

Wine Pairing with Alsatian Food

Hearty dishes, fresh ingredients, and a distinct fusion of French and German elements are characteristics of Alsatian cuisine. Savor the ideal balance of wine and food by pairing your wine tasting with a typical Alsatian dinner.

Disclosing the Winemaking Secrets

Discover the rich history and customs of winemaking in Alsace by visiting one of the region's many wine museums. Discover the special terroir, the careful methods used to grow grapes, and the craft of winemaking.

Sommelier Etiquette

Take advantage of the regional traditions and customs during wine tasting in Alsace. Chew slowly, letting the tastes meld together on your tongue with each sip. Ask questions and gain more knowledge about the wines you are tasting by interacting with the winemaker or sommelier.

A Guide to Organizing Your Wine Tasting Experience

Make your itinerary: Look up the locations and operating hours of the wineries you want to visit.

Schedule your tastings in advance: Especially during busy seasons, popular vineyards may demand reservations.

Pace yourself: Give each taste session enough time, and take pauses to enjoy the surrounding landscape.

Be aware of your palate: To guarantee an authentic impression of the wines, abstain from smoking and heavy food before your tastings.

Accept the experience: Take in the ambience, converse with the winemakers, and relish the customs and tastes of Alsatian wine.

Outdoor Adventures: Hiking and Cycling Routes

Situated between the Rhine River and the Vosges Mountains, Alsace presents a mesmerizing fusion of scenic splendor, cultural legacy, and delectable cuisine. Alsace offers a plethora of hiking and cycling trails, catering to the interests of outdoor lovers who wish to visit its picturesque villages, rolling hills, and vineyards.

Trails for Hikers of All Skill Levels

All skill levels of hikers and walkers can find something to suit them on Alsace's vast network of paths. The Hansi Trail in Riquewihr, a quaint village with half-timbered buildings, is a great place for leisurely strolls. Go into the Vosges Mountains for more strenuous hiking; paths like the Sentier des Roches and the

Haut-Koenigsbourg Castle Loop provide beautiful scenery and a tranquil atmosphere.

Riding a Cyclist Through Villages and Vineyards

bicycle enthusiasts will find Alsace to be a perfect location due to its mild topography and well-kept bicycle trails. Winding through the center of the region's vineyards, the 120-kilometer Véloroute du Vignoble offers possibilities for sampling local wines and scenic vistas. The path des Crêtes, a 70-kilometer path across the Vosges Mountains, offers breathtaking views and a sense of achievement for a more strenuous ride.

Uncovering Secret Treasures

For those with an adventurous spirit, Alsace has a wealth of undiscovered treasures just waiting to be found off the well-traveled paths. Take a trek along the Chemin du Bonheur, a trail renowned for its peace and breathtaking views. Alternatively, explore the captivating waterfalls found in the Vosges Mountains, like the Heidenbach and Échelle cascades.

Organizing Your Nature Experience

Take into account these useful suggestions to guarantee an unforgettable outdoor experience in Alsace:

Arrange your itinerary: Look into the bike routes and trails that meet your interests and degree of fitness.

Select the proper equipment: Bring appropriate apparel and footwear based on the terrain and weather.

Be ready for anything: Always have a map, a compass, and a first aid kit with you.

Conserve the environment: Take care around wildlife and leave no evidence of your visit.

Adopt the local way of life: Savor regional food, explore quaint towns, and become fully immersed in the area's distinctive history.

Charm and Hospitality of the Alestians

When you set out on your outdoor activities in Alsace, you'll come across the kindliness and hospitality that characterize the culture of the area. Savor the delicacies of the regional food, take in the beauty of this enchanted area, and spend time with other walkers and cyclists.

Exploring Strasbourg's Surroundings

The capital of France's Grand Est region, Strasbourg, is a mesmerizing city full of architectural beauty, vibrant culture, and historical charm. Travelers with discernment will find a tapestry of charming villages, undulating hills, and vineyards beyond the city's enchanted boundaries. Explore the environs of Strasbourg and get a taste of the magnificent landscapes, mouthwatering cuisine, and rich cultural legacy of the area.

Magical Villages Immortalized throughout Time

Cheryl: Enter the charming medieval village of Riquewihr, which is surrounded by vineyards. Wander the flower-adorned half-timbered cottages lining the cobblestone streets, and find quaint squares with statues

and fountains: Admire the Dolder Tower, dating back to the 13th century and representing the village's defenses, and pay a visit to the Hansi Museum, which features pieces by the well-known Alsatian artist.

Pathfinder: Travel to Kaysersberg, a hamlet steeped in medieval history, where the majestic Château de Kaysersberg stands as the village's crown. Stroll down the charming streets that are bordered by vibrant half-timbered homes that are decorated with bougainvillea and geraniums. Discover the village's defensive history by seeing the 13th-century Fortified Bridge. You can also explore the Renaissance masterpiece Town Hall, which is decorated with frescoes that reflect local tales.

Hermann Schein: Take a day trip to Eguisheim, a quaint community known for being the origin of Alsace's Grand Cru wines, which is tucked away among vineyards. Wander around the narrow alleyways that are dotted with half-timbered homes that have balconies full of flowers. Discover the ruins of the settlement's medieval defenses, the three gates, and the 12th-century Château du Haut-Koenigsbourg, which sits on a hill with views of the vineyards and village below.

In Stuttgart: Visit Mittelbergheim, a charming community tucked away at the base of Mont Sainte-Odile. Take in the beautifully restored half-timbered homes that are accented with vibrant flower displays. See the 13th-century Fortified Church of Saint-Pierre-et-Paul to learn about the community's medieval past, and stop by the Winzerhof, a Renaissance manor house turned museum highlighting the history of winemaking in the village.

Châteaut-Königsbourg Castle: An Elegant Stronghold Perched Above the Hills

Reach the summit of the Vosges Mountains to explore the magnificent Haut-Kœnigsbourg Castle, a castle from the 12th century that sits atop a hill with a view of the Alsace area. Imagine the castle's involvement in medieval conflicts and sieges as you explore its majestic ramparts, towers, and courtyards. Take in the opulent interiors of the castle, which are furnished with antique furniture, armor, and tapestries. Visit the museum to learn about the rich history of the castle and the lives of those who inhabited it, as well as its strategic significance. Climb the towers of the castle to get a beautiful overview over the neighboring villages, woodlands, and vineyards.

Deeply Soak in the Armor of Nature

Alpines Vosges: Explore the peaceful Vosges Mountains, a land of verdant forests, placid lakes, and undulating hills. Take energetic hikes along the lush paths that lead to scenic overlooks and hidden waterfalls. Ride your bike along picturesque routes that meander through quaint towns and vineyards. Alternatively, explore the abundant fauna of the area, encompassing deer, foxes, and wild boar.

Wine Road in Alsace: Trace the enticing 170-kilometer Alsace Wine Route, which meanders through the center of the region's vineyards. Explore the world of Alsatian wine and discover quaint villages, historic wineries, and stunning views. Participate in wine tastings at nearby vineyards to experience the flavors of Riesling, Sylvaner, Gewürztraminer, and Pinot Gris.

Forest of Haut-Königsbourg: Discover the enchanted Haut-Königsbourg Forest, a calm sanctuary with tall trees, colorful wildflowers, and peaceful streams. Explore the trails that wind through the forest to find secret glades and historic ruins. Alternatively, just lose yourself in the peace and quiet of the natural world while taking in the crisp air and hearing the melodies of the birds.

Explore Gastronomic Treasures

Culinary Arts: Take a culinary tour of Alsace and enjoy the rich culinary legacy of the area. Savor filling Alsatian cuisine like baeckeoffe, choucroute, and flammekueche. Try some of the famous cheeses from the area, such as Munster and Munstervals. Savor the delectable flavors of Alsatian desserts like tarte Tatin and kugelhopf.

Local Fairs and Markets: Take in the lively ambiance of nearby markets and fairs, where you may taste regional food.

CHAPTER 7: SHOPPER'S PARADISE

Strasbourg's Markets and Boutiques

In addition to its rich history, vibrant culture, and stunning architecture, Strasbourg, the enchanted capital of the Alsace region of France, entices discriminating visitors with its diverse assortment of markets and stores. With its vibrant flea markets and sophisticated designer boutiques, Strasbourg offers something for every taste and budget, turning shopping into an immersive experience that combines regional flair with contemporary design.

Traversing the Shopping Paradise of Strasbourg

Shopping in Downtown: Get lost in the center of Strasbourg's retail district, which is home to several boutiques and specialized shops in addition to department stores like Galeries Lafayette and Printemps. Explore the lively pedestrian zones of Rue Grande and Rue du 22 Novembre, where an abundance of gastronomic treats, fashion, accessories, and home décor can be found.

Fairs and Markets: Visit the many markets and fairs in the city to get a true sense of Alsace culture. Every Saturday morning, at Place de l'Etoile, the Marché de la Brocante is a treasure hunter's dream come true, brimming with vintage finds, antiques, and one-of-a-kind items. Savor locally grown vegetables and mouthwatering Alsatian treats at the Wednesday and Friday markets at the Marché de la Place Broglie, as well as the spectacular Christmas market, the Marché de

Noël, which turns the city into a wintry paradise.

Artisanal crafts and boutiques: Explore Strasbourg's artistic culture by perusing the quaint shops and ateliers dotted around the city. Discover gorgeous jewelry creations at Bijouterie Brandt, or visit Au Fil des Couleurs to lose yourself in the world of fine fabrics and home decor. Visit Atelier Hansi for a taste of Alsatian artistry. Here, you can purchase locally made souvenirs, textiles, and ceramics that are influenced by the history of the area.

Cost-effective Buying: Budget-conscious shoppers have a plethora of options in Strasbourg. Discover hidden treasures at reasonable costs by perusing the antique boutiques and thrift stores along Rue du Jeu des Quilles and Rue des Juifs. For deals on designer names, head to the Strasbourg outlets, which are situated just outside the city center.

Recommended Local Stores

Adopt local traditions: Say "Bonjour" and "Merci" to store owners when you enter and go.

Trade at consignment stores: It's normal to haggle over costs at the Marché de la Brocante, so don't be afraid to do so.

Adopt local craftspeople: Browse boutiques and ateliers for distinctive handcrafted goods, and don't forget to bring home a bit of Alsatian craftsmanship.

Arrange your shopping itinerary: To guarantee a productive and pleasurable shopping session, list all of your destinations.

Slightly pack: If you intend to buy large products, think about having them delivered right to your house.

Buying Conscientiously

Fair trade and sustainable practices are priorities for Strasbourg. Seek out regional companies that promote regional artists and obtain their supplies from ethical sources. For organic and fair-trade produce, visit the Marché Biologique des Halles, which is held every Wednesday and Saturday.

Strasbourg: An Unmatched Shopping Experience

Strasbourg provides a shopping experience that extends beyond the simple purchase of products thanks to its unique combination of old world charm and contemporary sensibility. It's a chance to take in the rich cultural diversity of the area, admire the artistry of regional craftspeople, and find the one-of-a-kind finds that turn Strasbourg into a shopping haven.

Unique Souvenirs to Bring Home

There is a hidden cache of one-of-a-kind mementos waiting to be unearthed in Strasbourg, beyond its charming streets, iconic locations, and mouthwatering cuisine. These mementos, which range from humorous reminders of the city's beauty to handcrafted Alsatian delights, will become treasured keepsakes of your time spent in this alluring area.

1. Wine from Alsace: World-class wines are known from Alsace, where the most well-known varietals are Riesling, Gewürztraminer, Pinot Gris, and Sylvaner. Take a bottle or two home to enjoy the local flavors and to share with loved ones.

2. Cookies Bredele: These delicious traditional Alsatian Christmas cookies make thoughtful gifts for family members or friends. Bredele cookies are adorned with elaborate patterns and flavored with hearty spices, offering a taste of Alsatian cuisine.

3. Gouldspeak: An essential component of Alsatian cooking is this strong, delicious cheese. Take home a wedge of Munster to eat on its own, as part of a cheese buffet, or mixed into substantial recipes.

4. Products Hanzi: These wacky mementos, which range from toys and household goods to pottery and fabrics, are inspired by the paintings of the well-known Alsatian artist Hansi and perfectly express the allure and splendor of the area.

5. Glasses of Alsace Wine: These green-base, long-stemmed glasses are made especially to bring out the flavor and aroma of Alsatian wines. Take a pair home to make wine-drinking more enjoyable.

6. Traditional Alsatian Costumes: Bring home little copies of traditional Alsatian costumes, which are embellished with colorful and detailed embellishments, to fully immerse oneself in the rich heritage of the area.

7. Artisan Wood Toys: Bring home handcrafted wooden toys, like animals, puzzles, and rocking pretzels, to experience the artistry of Alsatian craftsmen. Kids and adults alike will love these sentimental keepsakes.

8. Nearby Ceramics & Pottery: Alsatian ceramics and pottery are renowned for their exquisite designs and artistry. Select from an assortment of items, including bowls, vases, and mugs, to infuse your house with a hint of Alsatian charm.

9. Items with Stork Decorations: Alsace is associated with the stork, which stands for luck and fresh starts. Look for mementos with stork themes, such ornaments, keychains, and figurines, to add a bit of Alsatian symbolism to your house.

10. Handicrafts and Local Art: Take home one-of-a-kind artwork and crafts, such jewelry, paintings, and handwoven fabrics, to show your support for the neighborhood's creatives. These gems will act as physical remembrances of the artistic legacy of the area.

When you go shopping in Strasbourg, don't forget to enjoy the experience, pay attention to the skill of the local craftspeople, and select mementos that capture your own style and bring back happy memories of your stay in this charming city.

Shopping Districts for Every Budget

Strasbourg provides an array of shopping experiences to cater to all tastes and budgets, ranging from opulent department shops to little boutiques and lively markets. Strasbourg offers a unique experience for those looking for artisan things, local treasures, or high-end couture.

High-end and Designer Labels

Rue Grande: A hint of luxury can be added to your shopping experience with the high-end labels like Louis Vuitton, Hermès, and Cartier that line this sophisticated pedestrian strip.

Print-emps: This well-known department store caters to affluent customers with a wide assortment of designer clothing, makeup, and home decor.

Lafayette's Galeries: Fashion fans should not miss this classic department store, which features a carefully chosen selection of French and international brands.

In the Mid-Range

Nordweg 22 November: This bustling boulevard offers a blend of specialist shops, boutiques, and well-known brands at prices that are both stylish and reasonable.

Halles Place: There are stores, cafes, and market booths all around this central area, making for a bustling environment as you go shopping.

Juffs Road: This charming boulevard features a mix of modern businesses, vintage boutiques, and classic Alsatian shops to suit a wide variety of tastes.

Cost-effective Buying

La Brocante Marché: This flea market, which is held every Saturday morning at Place de l'Etoile, is a veritable gold mine of antiques, vintage discoveries, and unusual collectibles.

Outlets in Strasbourg: Shrewd shoppers will find a paradise in these outlet stores, which are conveniently located just outside the city center and offer savings on designer items.

Vintage boutiques and thrift stores: Discover the hidden treasures on Rue du Jeu des Quilles and Rue des Juifs, where you can find affordable, fashionable apparel, accessories, and home decor.

Crafts and Souvenirs Authentic to the Area

Atelier Hansi: This quaint shop features the creations of well-known Alsatian artist Hansi and provides a large selection of locally inspired souvenirs, handcrafted ceramics, and fabrics.

Workshops and Stores: Explore Strasbourg's artistic culture by perusing the quaint shops and ateliers dotted around the city. Discover gorgeous jewelry creations at Bijouterie Brandt, or visit Au Fil des Couleurs to lose yourself in the world of fine fabrics and home decor.

Noël Marché: The Marché de Noël turns the city into a wintry wonderland over the holiday season. Take a leisurely stroll among the illuminated stalls to discover distinctive handcrafted ornaments, Alsatian delights, and regional specialties.

Guides for Budget-Friendly Shopping

Arrange your shopping itinerary: To guarantee a productive and pleasurable experience, list all of your shopping destinations.

Carry reusable bags: Reduce your environmental impact and save extra charges by bringing your own shopping bags.

Appreciate local markets and fairs: Take in the true essence of Alsace while snagging deals at the many markets and festivals throughout the city.

Take into account used options: A wealth of fashionable and distinctive goods are available at reasonable costs in thrift stores and retro boutiques.

Have perseverance and patience: Take your time when shopping. Take your time looking over items, haggling over pricing at flea markets, and finding hidden treasures.

CHAPTER 8: NIGHTLIFE AND ENTERTAINMENT

Evening Strolls and Illuminated Landmarks

Strasbourg becomes a mesmerizing display of lights and shadows as the sun sets, unveiling a secret realm full of charm and enchantment. Take a nighttime stroll in the center of Strasbourg, where famous sites that are illuminated with colorful lights come to life under the starry sky.

A Wander Through Strasbourg's Illuminated Heart

Île du Grand: Start your evening stroll at Strasbourg's UNESCO World Heritage Site, the Grande Île, the city's historic core. Admire the majestic Cathédrale Notre-Dame, with its towering spires bathed in a warm, ethereal glow, as you meander around the cobblestone streets. Proceed to the Place de la Cathédrale, where the buildings in the area, lit up in amber and gold tones, create a captivating atmosphere.

French Petite: Pass under the Pont Neuf, a pedestrian bridge over the Ill River, and you'll arrive in the quaint Petite France neighborhood, named for its half-timbered homes with flower-filled balconies. As you stroll alongside the charming canals, you'll see the illuminated buildings' shimmering reflections, which create a mystical ambiance.

Vauban Barrage: Proceed on your stroll towards the Barrage Vauban, a colossal dam from the 17th century that comes alive at night with an amazing display of lights. An enthralling visual display is produced as the water flows down the dam and is lighted in a captivating swirl of colors.

L'Orangerie Park: Visit the peaceful green haven of Parc de l'Orangerie to get away from the bustle of the city. After twilight, stroll along the lit walks that are bordered by verdant trees and peaceful fountains, and take in the peaceful atmosphere of the park.

Outside the City Core

Tanneries Quarter: Go past the Grand Île to the Quartier des Tanneurs, a former industrial area turned lively center of entertainment and nightlife. Take a stroll down the Rue de la Bruyère, which is dotted with eateries, art galleries, and bars, and take in the vibrant atmosphere.

Neudorf: Discover the Neudorf neighborhood, which is renowned for its varied selection of cafes, restaurants, and music venues. Experience live music at one of the neighborhood's music halls, or simply unwind with a drink at a quaint pub while taking in the lively vibe of the area.

Alternative: Visit Kronenbourg, a medieval village just outside the city center, for a more traditional experience. Wander around the lit streets, which are bordered by old Alsatian homes, and take in this little suburb's genuine feel.

Guides for a Pleasurable Evening Walk

Dress comfortably: Put on shoes that are appropriate for walking on uneven surfaces and cobblestone streets.

Set your pace: Take your time, savor the beauty of the city, and let the ambience fill you.

Take a camera: Record the enthralling lights and make enduring recollections of your stroll in the evening.

Savor the regional cuisine: Stop at one of the numerous eateries or cafés along your path to savor a typical Alsatian meal.

Embrace the nightlife: Take advantage of the exciting nightlife of the city by attending live events or simply relaxing with a drink at a neighborhood bar.

Trendy Bars and Cafés

Strasbourg's lively nightlife comes to life as the sun sets, providing a wide selection of hip pubs and welcoming cafes to satisfy any taste. Immerse yourself in the vibrant atmosphere of Strasbourg and discover the distinct flavors and ambiance of its nightlife, from traditional Alsatian pubs to hipster hangouts.

Indie vibes and hipster hangouts

The Conduite Zero: Explore this unique pub, a sanctuary for creative types and music lovers. Savor DJ sets, live music events, and a lively vibe that draws a varied clientele.

The Abord Brothers: Take in the bohemian vibe of this quaint tavern, which is well-known for its welcoming atmosphere, attentive service, and assortment of Alsatian wines and craft brews from the area.

Discover Le Zocco: Nestled in a quaint courtyard, this hidden gem offers a distinctive fusion of Moroccan food, live music, and a laid-back vibe.

Original Flavors and Traditional Alsatian Pubs

At the Beef and the Cheval: Enter this 16th-century Alsatian bar and take in the atmosphere with its true authenticity. Savor robust Alsatian cuisine paired with a variety of regional wines and beers.

The Cheese Cave: Discover the world of cheese at this welcoming wine bar, which serves a wide assortment of French and Alsatian cheeses matched with excellent wines.

Bouchon Tire: Explore this authentic Alsatian tavern, renowned for its welcoming ambiance, mouthwatering flammekueche (flatbread from Alsace), and an extensive selection of regional beers.

Lounges and Cafés for a Calm Evening

L'entrée à emporter: Come to this literary-themed café to get away from the bustle of the city and read a selection of books while sipping wine or coffee.

Kammerzell House: Enter this old timber-framed house that has been turned into a quaint café and restaurant serving authentic Alsatian food in a lovely setting.

Aphrodite's Secrets: Savor the sweet delicacies and welcoming ambiance of this distinctive café, which is well-known for its assortment of hand-made pastries, teas, and chocolates.

Recommendations for Enjoying Strasbourg's Nightlife

Discover diverse neighborhoods: Go outside the city center to learn about the distinctive nightlife options in other areas.

Adopt local customs: Say "Bonjour" and "Merci" to waiters and bartenders.

Adopt local companies: For a true taste of Alsace, choose independently owned taverns and cafes.

Be aware of noise levels: Pay attention to the peace and quiet in residential areas, particularly at night.

Live Music and Cultural Performances

Strasbourg comes to life as the sun sets with a symphony of noises and a bright display of cultural events. Strasbourg offers a captivating fusion of innovation and history in its cultural landscape, which includes everything from modern theater shows to classic Alsatian music.

Take A Deep Dive Into the Beat of Classic Alsatian Music

La Tristeza: Discover the thrilling ambiance of La Laiterie, a renowned concert theater that presents a wide variety of musical performances by both local and international musicians.

Le Molodoï: Explore this small-scale venue that features upcoming artists and new musical styles. Take in a range of live music events, featuring genres such as electronic music, indie rock, jazz, and blues.

Django's Space: Experience jazz and swing music up close at L'Espace Django, a music venue and cultural hub that regularly hosts concerts, workshops, and jam sessions.

Accept the Magical Theatrics of Strasbourg's Stages:

Rhine Opera House: Enter the splendor of the Opéra National du Rhin, a well-known opera venue that presents a mesmerizing schedule of ballets, modern performances, and classical operas.

Théâtre National de Strasbourg: Enjoy a wide selection of plays, ranging from modern productions to timeless masterpieces, at the Théâtre National de Strasbourg.

The Strasbourg Opera: Explore this dynamic theater that presents modern plays and is renowned for its creative and provocative stagings.

Explore the Magical World of Cultural Events

Celebration of Music: On June 21, take part in Strasbourg's citywide festival of music as live performers fill the squares, streets, and venues, bringing the city to life.

Automne Festival: Experience the world of modern dance and performance art at the September and October Festival d'Automne, which features worldwide artists and their avant-garde works.

Marché de Noël: Take in the enchanted atmosphere of the Christmas markets, which are hosted throughout December. The air is filled with traditional Alsatian music, storytelling, and performances, making for a joyous and enchanting occasion.

Guides for Appreciating Live Music and Cultural Events in Strasbourg:

Reserve tickets ahead of time: To avoid disappointment, reserve your seats in advance for popular performances and events.

Verify regional listings: Consult local newspapers, websites, and cultural centers to stay informed about forthcoming events and performances.

Dress appropriately: Pick clothes that fit the venue and style of performance while still being comfortable.

Honor the artists and the audience by keeping the environment quiet and focused throughout the performances.

Embrace the many cultural offerings: To broaden your horizons, experiment with various musical and theatrical genres and styles.

CHAPTER 9: PRACTICAL TIPS AND RESOURCES

Essential Travel Apps

Technology may be an invaluable travel companion that enhances your exploration and ensures a seamless and comfortable trip to the charming city of Strasbourg. This carefully chosen list of must-have travel applications will make your trip to Strasbourg smooth and unforgettable.

1. Travel to Strasbourg: Accept the official Strasbourg Tourism app as your go-to resource for getting about the city. Get comprehensive details about accommodations, dining options, activities, and attractions—all of which are neatly arranged by area and category.

2. Red Cross Transports Strasbourg: Use the CTiS Transports Strasbourg app to receive real-time updates on public transportation. Making travel plans, monitoring bus and tram arrivals, and buying tickets straight from the app will make getting around the city easy.

3. Translated by Google: Use Google Translate to get around linguistic obstacles. Translate menus, signs, and conversations instantly to improve your cultural immersion and ensure smooth communication with locals.

4. Maps.me: Use Maps.me to explore Strasbourg offline. Get thorough maps of the city and its environs so you can confidently travel even in the absence of an internet connection.

5. The Knife: Use The Fork app to explore Strasbourg's gastronomic offerings. Make reservations, look through menus, and take advantage of special offers to guarantee a great meal.

6. AccuWeather : Use AccuWeather to stay up to date on the weather. Get precise weather predictions, notifications, and up-to-date information so you can plan ahead for any changes in the weather.

7. XE Exchange Rates: You can easily manage your finances by using the XE Currency Converter app. Track currency rates, convert currencies instantaneously, and keep up with market changes.

8. Map of WiFi: Use the Wi-Fi Map app to locate free Wi-Fi hotspots in Strasbourg. You may easily connect to the internet, staying in touch and sharing your experiences with family and friends.

9. VacationIt: Organize your trip schedule using TripIt. Enjoy a stress-free travel experience by importing the data of your hotel, reservations, and flights, and accessing a consolidated trip itinerary.

10. My Emergence SOS: Use the My SOS Emergency app to stay informed and protected. In an emergency, you may access crucial emergency contacts, get help in a variety of languages, and sound an SOS signal.

Recall that rather than taking the place of travel, technology is here to improve it. Seize the chance to engage with the community, fully immerse yourself in the culture, and make enduring experiences that go beyond the screen.

Safety Guidelines and Emergency Contacts

Although there isn't much crime in Strasbourg, it's still a good idea to exercise caution and pay attention to your surroundings. The following are some safety precautions to take:

Overall Security

- Keep an eye out for your possessions, particularly in crowded places.
- Refrain against carrying a lot of cash or valuables.
- Pay attention to your surroundings and refrain from going alone at night in dimly lit locations.
- Stay out of unmarked automobiles and take licensed taxis.
- Ask for assistance from a passerby or a local store or restaurant if you feel uneasy or threatened.

In Case of Emergency

- Fire Department: 18
- Police: 17
- Ambulance: 15
- SOS Médecins: 33 (0)8 20 33 20 33
- European Emergency Number: 112

Further Advice

Acquire some basic French vocabulary, including "Hello," "Au revoir," "Merci," and "S'il vous plaît" (please).

Bring a map with you so you can find your way around the city. Respect the traditions and customs of the area. Report a crime to the police right away if you have been the victim of one.

Remaining Secure in Strasbourg

Be mindful of your surroundings: Be vigilant about your possessions, particularly in busy places like train stations and tourist destinations.

Avoid carrying large amounts of cash: Opt for a credit card or traveler's checks instead.

Be wary of pickpockets: Exercise extra caution in busy areas and store your valuables in a secure location.

Be mindful of scams: Exercise caution when approaching strangers on the street who offer to assist you with something, like exchanging money.

Avoid driving after drinking: France has a 0.5 mg/l legal blood alcohol limit.

Respect local traditions: When visiting places of worship, dress modestly.

Transportation Safety

Be cautious when boarding and exiting trams: Hold on to the railings and be aware of your surroundings.

Take licensed taxis: Avoid getting into unmarked cars.

Be mindful of your belongings on public transportation: Keep your belongings in sight and avoid leaving them unattended.

Calls for Emergencies

- Department of Fire: 18
- Police: 17
- Ambulance: 15
- European Emergency Number: 112
- SOS Médecins: 33 (0)8 20 33 20 33

You may contribute to a safe and happy vacation to Strasbourg by paying attention to your surroundings and adhering to these safety precautions.

Sustainable Travel Practices

In order to minimize your influence on the environment and maximize your vacation experience, think about implementing sustainable practices into your itinerary as you set off for the charming city of Strasbourg. These environmentally friendly decisions will seamlessly combine discovery and environmental responsibility with your trip to Strasbourg.

1. Adopt the Public Transit System: By taking advantage of Strasbourg's effective public transit system, you can reduce your carbon footprint while taking in the vibrant ambiance of the city. The city's network of trams, buses, and the Vélostras bike-sharing program make getting around easy and let you explore its many districts and landmarks while leaving the least amount of environmental damage behind.

2. Select Accommodations with Ecological Obligations: Choose lodgings that put an emphasis on sustainability, such as those with waste management programs, water conservation measures, and energy-efficient methods. You can urge the hospitality industry to adopt sustainable practices by patronizing eco-conscious hotels and guesthouses.

3. Explore Local Delights by Bike or Foot: Take a stroll or a bike ride through the local markets, cafes, and restaurants to get a taste of Strasbourg's vibrant food scene. This not only lessens your dependency on transportation but also lets you enjoy the charm of the city and find undiscovered treasures as you go.

4. Encourage Local and Sustainable Enterprises: Make it a priority to buy food, crafts, and souvenirs from regional suppliers and artists. By patronizing neighborhood businesses, you lessen the environmental effect of mass-produced goods, boost the local economy, and help preserve traditional ways of doing things.

5. Reduce Trash and Recycle Ethically: Consider reducing the amount of waste you produce by using reusable shopping bags, food containers, and water bottles. Make use of the city's recycling resources to properly dispose of your waste, supporting Strasbourg's efforts to maintain a sustainable environment.

6. Discover Green Areas and Value Nature: Enjoy parks, gardens, and natural places as a way to embrace Strasbourg's dedication to urban green spaces. Explore the Ill River promenade, the Jardin Botanique, and the Parc de l'Orangerie, letting nature enhance your discovery and support the ecological equilibrium of the city.

7. Select Eco-Friendly Exercises: Choose eco-friendly activities when you can, including hiking in the Vosges Mountains, cycling on beautiful routes, or attending eco-friendly events and workshops. These encounters support Strasbourg's dedication to sustainable tourism while also strengthening your bond with the area's natural beauty.

8. Decrease Energy Use: During your visit, adopt energy-saving habits including putting away lights and appliances when not in use, setting thermostats to comfortable levels, and selecting energy-efficient accommodations.

9. Be a Responsible Traveler: To guarantee a peaceful experience for both locals and other visitors, respect local customs and traditions, dress appropriately for cultural situations, and reduce noise pollution.

10. Share Your Sustainable Journey : Talk about your environmentally friendly travel experiences with others to encourage friends and family to follow in your footsteps and help create a more conscientious travel culture.

You can lessen your environmental effect and deepen your enjoyment of Strasbourg's natural beauty and cultural legacy by implementing these sustainable habits into your travels. This will benefit the place you hold dear.

Q&A Section: Common Traveler Inquiries

Here are some of the most common queries from visitors visiting Strasbourg as you organize your trip:

Overall inquiries

When is the ideal time to travel to Strasbourg?

All year long, Strasbourg is a lovely place to visit. While the fall and winter months give a quaint festive atmosphere, especially during the Christmas market season, the spring and summer months are best for outdoor city exploration.

How can I travel to Strasbourg?

Direct flights are available from Strasbourg Entzheim International Airport (SXB) to major cities in Europe. As an alternative, there are other European locations from which you can take a train to Strasbourg.

What is the Strasbourg currency?

The euro (€) is the accepted form of payment in Strasbourg.

In what language is Strasbourg spoken?

Although French is the official language of Strasbourg, several residents also speak Alsatian German. In tourist locations, English is generally understood.

Questions about Accommodation

Where in Strasbourg should I stay?

There are several lodging alternatives in Strasbourg to fit every taste and budget. For those who prefer to be in the thick of things, the city center is a terrific option, while the Petite France neighborhood offers a cozier, more traditional setting.

How much does lodging in Strasbourg cost?

The cost of lodging in Strasbourg varies based on the kind of lodging, the area, and the time of year. For a hotel room, you should generally budget between €50 and €200 or more each night.

Questions About Transportation

How can I navigate Strasbourg?

The public transportation system in Strasbourg is quite effective and comprises of buses, trams, and a scheme for sharing bikes. It is also rather easy to stroll around the city because of its walkability.

Is it possible to hail a cab in Strasbourg?

Indeed, there are plenty of cabs in Strasbourg. You can phone a taxi company or hail a cab on the street.

Does Strasbourg have Uber?

Indeed, Uber is available in Strasbourg.

Questions about Sightseeing:

What sights in Strasbourg are definitely worth seeing?

There are many things to see and do in Strasbourg, such as the Barrage Vauban, the Palais Rohan, the Petite France neighborhood, and the Cathédrale Notre-Dame.

How much time should I spend in Strasbourg?

In two or three days, you may see the majority of Strasbourg's attractions. Still, you could explore the city for a week or longer if you want to get a better sense of it.

Additional Queries

What are some typical foods from Alsace?

Traditional Alsatian fare includes thick stews like baeckeoffe, choucroute (sausage and sauerkraut), and flammekueche (thin tart with a variety of toppings).

What mementos from Strasbourg can I buy locally?

Glassware, ceramics, and Christmas ornaments made in Hansi are a few of the regional mementos available in Strasbourg.

What are some suggestions for Strasbourg money-saving?

CHAPTER 10: YOUR STRASBOURG ITINERARY

One-Day Whirlwind Tour

Strasbourg is a fascinating city full of architectural wonders, cultural treasures, and delectable food. It is influenced by both French and German culture. Even a quick day trip can give you a sense of its alluring character, however a multi-day tour would definitely uncover its many facets. With this fast-paced schedule, you'll see the best of the city and make the most of your limited time.

Awaken to History and Architectural Magnificence

1. Saint-Germain-de- Strasbourg Cathedral: Start your day with the magnificent

Cathédrale Notre-Dame, located in the core of Strasbourg's historical district. See its gothic grandeur, ascend its tower for sweeping city vistas, and be in awe of the complex workings of the astronomical clock.

2. District of Petite France: Take a leisurely stroll around the charming Petite France neighborhood, which is home to half-timbered homes, cobblestone lanes, and canals. Take picture-perfect pictures of the covered bridges and enjoy the quaint atmosphere.

3. Rohan Pallais: Proceed to the Palais Rohan, a former seat of the episcopate that features a fusion of Classical and Baroque design. Discover its museums, such as the Decorative Arts Museum and the Museum of Fine Arts.

Afternoon: Sophisticated Cuisine and Historical Treasures

1. Alsatian meal: Savor a hearty Alsatian meal, with regional favorites like thick beef and vegetable stew baeckeoffe, choucroute (sauerkraut with pork and sausages), and flammekueche (a thin tart with varied toppings).

2. Boat Tour Around Battambang: Take a Batorama boat excursion to see Strasbourg from a different angle. Admire the city's architectural treasures from a watery vantage point as you glide among the canals.

3. The Parliament of Europe: See the European Parliament, one of the most important sites in the city. Investigate the displays to learn more about how the European Union operates.

Evening: Scenic Views and Enchanting Ambiance

1. Sit Kléber here: Head to Strasbourg's central plaza, Place Kléber, as the sun starts to set. Enjoy a traditional Alsatian pastry, take in the lively ambiance, and pay homage to the statue of General Kléber.

2. Vauban Barrage: Take a stroll beside the Barrage Vauban, a charming dam that provides breathtaking views of the Petite France neighborhood and the Ill River. Take mesmerizing pictures of the setting sun as the city lights start to come on.

3. At a Conventional Winstub for Dinner: Finish your fast-paced tour with a traditional Alsatian meal at a quaint winstub (a traditional Alsatian pub). Savor the friendly ambiance, hearty cuisine, and local wines.

With this one-day itinerary, you can enjoy Strasbourg's historical charm, architectural marvels, and cultural richness. It offers a thorough overview of the must-see sights. Even though a day might not be enough to properly experience Strasbourg's charms, it certainly acts as a mouthwatering introduction that makes you want to come back for a closer look.

Weekend Getaway Recommendations

Strasbourg is a perfect place to spend a weekend escape. Strasbourg has something to offer any kind of traveler, whether they're looking for gastronomic treats, historical treasures, or leisurely strolls.

Soak Up the Historical Charm of Strasbourg

1. Saint-Germain-de- Strasbourg Cathedral: Admire this magnificent example of Gothic architecture, with its soaring spires and minute details that perfectly capture the opulence of medieval design. Reach the platform for sweeping views of the city.

2. French petite: Stroll around this charming neighborhood and enter a world straight out of a fairy tale. Admire the half-timbered homes that border the canals and take picture-perfect moments with the covered bridges set against cobblestone streets.

3. Rohan Pallais: Visit the former episcopal palace, Palais Rohan, to learn more about the cultural tapestry of the city. Discover its museums, which hold priceless items including ornamental antiquities and excellent arts.

Revel in the Tastes of Alsace

1. Culinary Treasures from Alsatians: Savor the flavors of Alsatian cuisine as you go on a culinary journey. Taste flammekueche, a thin tart covered with a variety of delicacies, or choucroute, a substantial dish of sausages, pork, and sauerkraut.

2. Boat Tour Around Battambang: Ride the Ill River and take in Strasbourg's architectural treasures from a different angle. Enjoy Alsatian wines and local specialties while cruising and taking in the stunning views.

3. Sit Kléber here: Take in the lively vibe of Place Kléber, the main square of Strasbourg. Take in the history of the city by admiring the statue of General Kléber, and maybe treat yourself to a typical Alsatian pastry.

Relax in the Enchanting Ambiance of Alsace

1. Vauban Barrage: Capture mesmerizing sunset vistas at Barrage Vauban, a charming dam with breathtaking views of the Petite France neighborhood and the Ill River. Enjoy the peaceful atmosphere as you stroll down the promenade and the city lights start to sparkle.

2. Classic Winstub: Finish your weekend trip with a traditional Alsatian meal in a little winstub. Savor the friendly atmosphere, robust cuisine like the meaty beef and vegetable stew baeckeoffe, and the local wines.

The charm of Strasbourg reaches far beyond this plan, urging you to come back and do more exploring. Strasbourg provides a fantastic weekend vacation experience, whether you choose to explore its museums, meander through its quaint squares, or just take in the lively atmosphere.

Extended Stay Adventures

Strasbourg is a storehouse of cultural treasures, architectural marvels, and delectable food. It is a city where French and German influences coexist. A quick tour can give you an idea of what it's like, but a longer stay will allow you to really experience its alluring allure. Set out on an adventure to discover the city's lesser-known areas, indulge in its delectable cuisine, and take in its thriving cultural scene.

Exploring the Architectural Magnificence of Strasbourg

1. Saint-Germain-de- Strasbourg Cathedral: Take a day to explore this Gothic masterpiece and take in all of its beautiful elements, including the stained glass windows. Climb the tower to see sweeping city views and to see the fascinating astronomical clock in action.

2. District of Petite France: Explore the charming neighborhood of Petite France, where time appears to stand still. Take in the picturesque atmosphere while seeing the half-timbered homes that line the canals and taking famous pictures of the covered bridges.

3. Rohan Pallais: Enjoy a cultural immersion in the three-museum-housed Palais Rohan, a former episcopal palace. Discover the many facets of Strasbourg's rich past by visiting the Museum of Fine Arts, the Museum of Decorative Arts, and the Archaeological Museum.

Delicious Foods and Deep Cultural Immersion

1. Culinary Arts of Algeria: Explore Alsace's culinary customs and indulge in local delicacies like baeckeoffe, choucroute, and flammekueche. Discover the genuine tastes and friendly service that characterize Alsatian food by visiting the neighborhood markets, bakeries, and dining establishments.

2. Boat Tour Around Battambang: Take a leisurely boat ride down the Ill River to see Strasbourg's famous sites from a different angle. As you ride down the scenic canals, take in the architectural treasures, relax and enjoy the fine wines and specialties of Alsace.

3. The Parliament of Europe: Learn about the European Parliament's influence on European policy by immersing yourself in the realm of international politics there. Take in the displays, go to a discussion open to the public, and learn about the inner workings of this important organization.

Outside the City: Discovering Strasbourg's Surroundings

1. The Vosges Mountain Range: Explore the Vosges Mountains, a breathtakingly beautiful natural haven. Take a hike through verdant forests, find quaint settlements, and take in breath-taking vistas of the surrounding countryside.

2. The Wine Road: Travel the Alsace Wine Route and sample the famous wines of the area from vineyards tucked away in charming villages and rolling hills. Take in wine tastings, visit nearby wineries, and discover the rich winemaking customs of the area.

3. Germany's Baden-Baden: For a day excursion to Baden Baden, a picturesque spa town renowned for its thermal springs, tasteful architecture, and lively cultural scene, cross the border into Germany. Savor German cuisine, tour the town's historic core, and indulge in restorative spa treatments.

Long-Term Lodging: A House Apart from a House

1. Apartment Rentals: For a more comfortable extended visit, think about renting an apartment. You can pick from a range of alternatives, from roomy apartments to comfortable studios, so you can be sure you have the ideal place to relax and feel at home.

2. Hotels with Extended Stays: Choose extended-stay hotels, which offer cozy lodging, kitchenettes, and frequent extras like business centers and laundry services. These establishments are designed to accommodate guests staying for longer periods of time.

3. House Stays: Select a homestay to fully immerse yourself in the culture and experience the friendliness and warmth of the people that live in Strasbourg. Get a deeper grasp of the city's culture, savor real Alsatian cuisine, and get insider information on nearby sites.

Take Up the Beat of Strasbourg Living

1. Festivals and Markets: Take in the lively ambiance of Strasbourg's festivals and markets. Take advantage of the festive atmosphere at one of the many cultural and food festivals conducted all year long, or visit the Christmas markets.

2. Events and Performances in the Area: Take in the local shows and events to fully experience Strasbourg's many cultural offerings. Experience the lively street acts that frequently occupy the city's squares, see plays at the Comédie de Strasbourg, or take in classical music concerts at the Palais des Fêtes.

3. Digging Into Communities: Go beyond the popular tourist destinations and discover the varied neighborhoods in Strasbourg. Find hidden treasures, sample regional cuisine at neighborhood eateries, and converse with the amiable residents to get a better sense of the city's true essence.

Long-Term Visit Adventures: Immense Recollections

Allow yourself to be enchanted by Strasbourg's alluring beauty, rich cultural legacy, and gracious hospitality as you begin your prolonged stay there. Explore its undiscovered treasures, indulge in its delectable cuisine, and become fully immersed in the lively pace of the community.

As you explore more of this alluring city, make lifelong memories that will stay with you, and depart with a heart full of treasured recollections and

CONCLUSION

Final Thoughts and Reflections

As you say goodbye to Strasbourg, a city whose alluring beauty, rich cultural diversity, and gracious hospitality have enhanced your spirit, pause to consider the lasting impression it has made on your travel experiences. Strasbourg has revealed its layers of history, culture, and gastronomic delights, leaving you with a treasure trove of experiences. From the breathtaking majesty of its Gothic cathedral to the quaint ambience of its half-timbered buildings surrounding the canals.

Recall the charming Petite France neighborhood, where you may feel time stand still as you stroll along its charming streets, taking in the famous covered bridges and shooting timeless images. Remember being in awe of the Cathedrale Notre-Dame de Strasbourg's elaborate machinery and the passage of time during the fascinating astronomical clock performance?

Savor the rich fragrances and filling flavors of flammekueche, choucroute, and baeckeoffe to relive the delights of Alsatian cuisine. Imagine yourself on a Batorama boat tour that glides along the Ill River, seeing the city's architectural treasures from a distinct vantage point, and indulging in wines and delicacies from Alsace.

Treasure the time you spent discovering the European Parliament and learning about the importance of global cooperation as well as the inner workings of this powerful organization. Remember the peacefulness of the Barrage Vauban, where you watched the city lights glimmer as they reflected in the Ill River and took beautiful sunset panoramas?

Cherish the memories of your trips outside of the city center, whether it be hiking in the picturesque Vosges Mountains, exploring Baden-Baden's allure, or taking a wine tour along the Alsace Wine Route. Accept the kindness and warmth of everyone you met, from amiable store owners to hospitable residents, who enhanced your visit by sharing their knowledge and experiences.

Bring back the spirit of Strasbourg, a city that has artfully combined its German and French roots to create a singular tapestry of culture, architecture, and gastronomic pleasures, as your adventure comes to a close. Long after you've left, let the memory of its charming streets, classic sites, and friendly people tempt you to come back and do more exploring.

I am grateful that you are traveling through Strasbourg with me. I hope this thorough guide has been your devoted companion, offering advice, suggestions, and ideas to help you plan your own unique trip to Strasbourg.

How to Stay Connected and Share Your Strasbourg Experience

When your trip to Strasbourg comes to an end, full of memories and a desire to share them with the world, think about the different ways you might keep in touch and interact with other tourists and fans of this fascinating city.

1. Portals on Social Media: Make use of social media sites such as Facebook, Instagram, and Twitter to provide your network with suggestions, thought-provoking stories, and visually appealing images. To reach a larger audience, use relevant hashtags such as #StrasbourgFrance #AlsaceAdventures #StrasbourgTravel.

2. Forums and Blogs about Travel: Use a travel blog or forum to go into further depth about your experiences in Strasbourg.

Compose in-depth pieces that showcase the city's best features, undiscovered attractions, and insider advice. Interact with other travelers by responding to their inquiries and sharing your knowledge.

3. **Virtual Communities and Associations:** Become a member of online forums and communities devoted to travel, particularly to Strasbourg. Talk about your experiences, take part in conversations, and get fresh viewpoints from other travelers who are as excited about exploring as you are.

4. **Photography Exhibitions and Contests:** Send in your striking images of Strasbourg for exhibits and photography competitions. Through the lens of your camera, share your artistic perspective of the city, highlighting its beauty and distinct character.

5. Local Occasions and Social Gatherings: Participate in regional travel and photography-related activities and networking opportunities. Make connections with other enthusiasts, exchange stories, and grow your network of like-minded people.

6. Citizen Engagement and Volunteer Opportunities: Think about lending your time and expertise to Strasbourg-based organizations that support travel and cross-cultural interactions. By imparting your expertise and enthusiasm for the city, you may positively influence the surrounding community.

7. Artistic Expressions and Creative Storytelling: Write poetry, short stories, or even music inspired by your experiences in Strasbourg to unleash your creativity. Present your own viewpoint while encapsulating the spirit of the city in a variety of artistic mediums.

8. Exchanging Memorabilia and Presents: Give your loved ones back home postcards, mementos, or even personalized photo albums or artwork to commemorate your time spent in Strasbourg. Spread the word about this fascinating place and let others experience the thrill of your trips.

9. Suggested Word-of-Mouth Activities: Talk to friends, family, and coworkers, and give your honest account of your experiences in Strasbourg. Talk about this fascinating city's hidden treasures and cultural diversity to entice others to visit.

10. Internet Evaluations and Stars: On travel-related websites and platforms, such as Booking.com, TripAdvisor, and Google Maps, leave favorable evaluations and ratings. Give prospective tourists your insights so they may plan their trip to Strasbourg with more knowledge.

Recall that telling others about your experiences in Strasbourg serves a dual purpose: it preserves your memories, allows you to relive the exciting and illuminating moments, and encourages others to do their own Strasbourg journeys.

Printed in Great Britain
by Amazon